The Power of Myth
in Literature and Film

The Power of Myth in Literature and Film

Selected Papers from the Second Annual
Florida State University Conference on
Literature and Film

Edited by Victor Carrabino

Associate Editors:
Peter Ruppert
H. Peter Stowell

A Florida State University Book
UNIVERSITY PRESSES OF FLORIDA
Tallahassee 1980

University Presses of Florida, the agency of the
State of Florida's university system for the publi-
cation of scholarly and creative works, operates
under policies adopted by the Board of Regents.
Its offices are located at 15 Northwest 15th Street,
Gainesville, Florida 32603.

Published through the Imprint Series,
UMI Monographs.
Produced and distributed by
University Microfilms International
Ann Arbor, Michigan 48106

Library of Congress Cataloging in Publication Data

**Florida State University Conference on Literature
and Film, 2d, Tallahassee, 1977.**
The power of myth in literature and film.

"A Florida State University book."
Includes bibliographies and index.
1. Myth in literature—Congresses. 2. Myth in motion
pictures—Congresses.   I. Carrabino, Victor. II. Title.
PN56.M94F5 1977   791.43'09'0915   80-21998
ISBN 0-8130-0673-2

For DANIELLE

CONTENTS

Preface

As a result of psychoanalytical studies, largely those of Freud and Jung, myth has been a significant topic in literary criticism. Myth has been correlated with the unconscious faculty of man, and myths have enabled man to deal face to face with the manifestations and knowledge of his unconscious, whether in dreams, behavior, or artistic output. As Erich Fromm wrote, "myth is a message from ourselves to ourselves, a second secret language which enables us to treat inner as if outer event."

Whether we understand myth as an expression of the conscious mind or of the unconscious, as sacred, psychic, individual, or political paradigm, we must come to recognize it as a fact of our literature and consequently of our lives. Our lives are shaped to some degree by the extent to which we indulge individually in myth-making efforts.

This collection of essays is the result of a conference sponsored by the Comparative Literature Circle of Florida State University in January, 1977, on the topic "Old Gods-New Heroes: The Power of Myth in Literature and Film."

The first three essays provide theoretical discussions of the totemic literary approach and its relevance to modern literary and filmic art. The essays that follow demonstrate various applications of myth criticism to specific literary works and films.

We would like to take this opportunity to express our appreciation to Dr. Robert O. Lawton, Vice-President for Academic Affairs, for his long-standing support of the Comparative Literature Circle's annual conferences. Our sincere thanks also go to Dr. Robert Johnson, Dean of Graduate Studies and Research, whose initial help and encouragement have been instrumental in the formulation of this project.

Finally, we would like to express our appreciation to the contributors to this volume, who have been patient and willing to make necessary changes as requested for the final form.

And, our special thanks go to Ms. Diana Bourdon for the typing of the manuscript and for her suggestions toward improvement of the finished product.

--V.C.

FROM THE SUBLIME TO THE ABSURD:

"OF IMAGINATION ALL COMPACT"

Anne Paolucci

I take my title--or part of it at any rate--from
the speech of Theseus in A Midsummer Night's Dream,
after he has heard much lovers' talk. "'Tis
strange," says Hippolyta in the opening lines of
Act V of Shakespeare's play, "that these lovers
speak of." And Theseus--the cool, clear, and calm
voice of common sense--replies:

> More strange than true. I never may believe
> These antique fables nor these fairy toys.
> Lovers and madmen have such seething brains,
> Such shaping fantasies, that apprehend
> More than cool reason ever comprehends.
> The lunatic, the lover, and the poet
> Are of imagination all compact.
> One sees more devils than vast hell can hold:
> That is the madman. The lover, all as
>   frantic,
> Sees Helen's beauty in a brow of Egypt.

After the lunatic and the lover, combining the fantasies of their seething brains in his fables and
fairy toys, comes the poet, for whom Shakespeare
writes this unsurpassed ars poetica:

The poet's eye, in a fine frenzy rolling,
Doth glance from heaven to earth, from earth
      to heaven;
And as imagination bodies forth
The forms of things unknown, the poet's pen
Turns them to shapes, and gives to airy
      nothing
A local habitation and a name.
Such tricks hath strong imagination
That, if it would but apprehend some joy,
It comprehends some bringer of that
      joy. . . .   (V, 1-20)

The voice of Theseus, the voice of poetry's own
self-denying common sense, is of course--in our
literary tradition--as old as Oedipus, who blasted
the Delphic Oracle and won the throne of Thebes by
applying reason to demolish the myth and mystery of
the Sphinx. But Oedipus' rationality went on to
demolish itself as well, so that what little
mystery there had been in the Sphinx was absurdly
absorbed in the far greater mystery and oracular
ambiguity of Oedipus himself. In taking flight
from the truth of Delphi, Oedipus had absurdly run
himself headlong into the fate he had sought to
avoid. Such is the fate of reason when it seeks,
in the name of reason, to be rid of poetry--which
is reason's highest, soundest intuition, some say.
Perhaps that is a paradox we should keep in mind
through this discussion of old gods and new heroes
and the enduring power of myth. There will always
be gods. They will always be wanted--with a price
on their heads--dead or alive. The names and the
descriptions will change--from blind fate just out
of chaos through battling titans to everlasting
savior and prince of peace and back again--according
to our convictions and aberrations, our wisdom and
ignorance; but there will always be gods.
    Some years ago I wrote a poem which keeps going
through my head. I'd like to quote it--with
apologies of course, especially coming so soon
after Shakespeare!--but I would like to quote it
because it expresses the kind of mood, I think,
which we find in many of our latter-day saints,
poets, and writers, who have become deities in their
own right, filling the vacuum. We know how Sartre
exhumed the myth of Oedipus to condemn the old gods

and exalt his own modern man-centered myth; my poem
is called "Poetry Reading" and goes like this:

> The gods are dead.
> Long live the bearded Greeks
> Bristling in their teeth,
> Chewing crumbs lodged there
> From Olympian feasts.
> Doric legs prop up
> The temple of words
> Where silent worshippers adore.
> From Delphi comes word
> The oracle has shut down
> For an indeterminate time
> While renovations go on.
> How does one go about telling this
> To a full house?
> Refund the money and apologize?
> Keep it, and your pleasure too!
> How inconsiderate the dead can be,
> Leaving their masks behind
> In the portico! It's all so confusing
> Unless one follows the celebrants
> Each to his own garret,
> And sees them eating peaches over the sink
> At midnight.

All of us crave deities in this prosaic age, and
since the skies have closed down on us in the modern
world (who hears the music of the spheres Dante
heard?) we mold our gods in our own image. Some
modern poets have felt the loss keenly. James
Thomson, the author of what is perhaps the most pes-
simistic poem in any language (as George Saintsbury
suggested), saw the vision of rationalist despair in
truly Dantesque terms. His City of Dreadful Night
carries three captions to set its mood: one from
Dante and two from Italy's great myth-making poet of
despair, Giacomo Leopardi. The city is a mighty
Babylon--New York, London, Paris, Rome--and it
towers gloomily on the edge of hell, though it
doesn't believe in hell. Dante's line--"per me si
va nella città dolente"--is therefore an appropriate
caption. Yet we are not in Dante's universe, with
its nest of moving skies, contained finitely in the
light and love of God. The quotations from
Leopardi--one from "Canto notturno" ("Night Song")

and "Coro dei Morti" ("Chorus of the Mummies")--
suggest how far removed we are from that universe.
In the lines quoted, Leopardi describes the motions
of heavenly bodies with Dantesque precision but to
an opposite purpose. Nature's endlessly repeated
motions snake back on themselves absurdly, so that
death--as the mummies know--is at least a rest from
repeated, active absurdity, however meaningless it
too may otherwise be. Thomson in his City gives
Dantesque expression to Leopardian despair, thereby
making it imaginatively or mythically his own. But
his darkness is deeper than Leopardi's. For a
moment, like Leopardi--and like Matthew Arnold in
"Dover Beach"--Thomson too is tempted to salvage
and embrace one last hope in that dreadful city of
night: human love. But that too is finally sacri-
ficed before the sunless 'Melancolia'--patroness,
Queen, and mythological symbol of his wasteland
metropolis. In a lovely short poem, called simply
"Proem," Thomson thus telescopes past, present, and
future, echoing Shakespeare's Theseus:

> O antique fables! Beautiful and bright
> And joyous with the joyous youth of yore;
> O antique fables! for a little light
> Of that which shineth in you evermore,
> To cleanse the dimness from our weary eyes,
> And bathe our old world with a new surprise
> Of golden dawn entrancing sea and shore.
> We stagger under the enormous weight
> Of all the heavy ages piled on us,
> With all their grievous wrongs inveterate,
> And all their disenchantments dolorous,
> And all the monstrous tasks they have
>   bequeathed;
> And we are stifled with the airs they
>   breathed;
> And read in theirs our doom calamitous.
>
> Our world is all stript naked of their dreams;
> No deities in sky or sun or moon,
> No nymphs in woods and hills and seas and
>   streams;
> Mere earth and water, air and fire, their
>   boon;
> No God in all our universe we trace,

No heaven in the infinitude of space,
No life beyond death--coming not too soon.

Our souls are stript of their illusions sweet,
Our hopes at best in some far future years
For others, not ourselves; whose bleeding feet
Wander this rocky waste where broken spears
And bleaching bones lie scattered on the sand;
Who know WE shall not reach the Promised Land;
Perhaps a mirage glistening through our tears.

And if there be this Promised Land indeed,
Our children's children's children's heritage,
Oh, what a prodigal waste of precious seed,
Of myriad myriad lives from age to age,
Of woes and agonies and blank despairs,
Through countless cycles, that some fortunate
      heirs
May enter, and conclude the pilgrimage!

But if it prove a mirage after all!
Our last illusion leaves us wholly bare,
To bruise against Fate's adamantine wall,
Consumed or frozen in the pitiless air;
In all our world, beneath, around, above,
One only refuge, solace, triumph--Love,
Sole star of light in infinite black despair.

O antique fables! beautiful and bright,
And joyous with the joyous youth of yore;
O antique fables! for a little light
Of that which shineth in you evermore,
To cleanse the dimness from our weary eyes
And bathe our old world with a new surprise
Of golden dawn entrancing sea and shore.

For Thomson even the triumph of love is an empty,
dark victory, as we said. Yet what the great critic
and philosopher Giovanni Gentile wrote of Leopardi
applies also to Thomson: both of them, in their
poetic rendering of the chaotic darkness of the
modern world, found and traced the divinity in
themselves. In their total commitment to despair
they represent, paradoxically, the moment of
poetry's vernal solstice, when things seem to stand
still on the brink of eternal darkness, before the
world grows light again.

There have been several such solstices in our
cultural history. Particularly in the chronicles
of gods and heroes there have been cycles of descent
from the sublimest heights into the depths of an
absurd--dark and chaotic--that turns out to be a
creative new beginning. For as Saturn says in
Keats' <u>Hyperion</u> after his son Zeus, aided and
abetted by Pluto and Neptune (I'm mixing the Greek
and Latin names), has dethroned him:

>   "But cannot I create?
>   Cannot I form? . . .
>   Where is another chaos? Where?"--That word
>   Found way unto Olympus, and made quake
>   The rebel three.

From the sublime to the absurd, and a spiraling off
to a new transcendence for the start of another
cycle--that seems to be the repeated course of
creative myth-making, which needs its depths of
chaos as much as it needs its soaring heavens and
all the things of time, in between.
   With that, we are already talking Homer and
Hesiod. The power of myth in literature and film
is, of course, a function of time, of Cronos.
Certainly the world since Homer and Hesiod has had
ample time and opportunity to give birth to new
myths. Yet it is a remarkable fact that those
first introduced into literature by Homer and Hesiod
have survived so extraordinarily well that even in
their most subtle transformations, subjected to all
kinds of analyses in an effort to unmask their
profoundest secrets, there has not been much room
for new births of more powerful myths to displace
them.
   Christianity, of course, transformed them radically, but it was a superhuman feat. Even so, the
best poets and writers of Christendom have felt the
need to associate in some way the Greek and
Christian written legacies. Dante especially saw
the development of poetry as well as of political
history and religious revelation as a long preparation for the "matter" of his poem, in which the
providential missions of Aeneas, on the Greco-Roman
side, and of St. Paul, on the Hebraic-Christian
side, are joined. "I am not Aeneas, I'm not Paul"--
<u>Io</u> <u>non</u> <u>Enea,</u> <u>io</u> <u>non</u> <u>Paolo</u> <u>sono</u>--says Dante at the

start of his epic journey beyond the grave; but
events prove that he is indeed both. Every step of
the way in the Commedia (but particularly in the
second canticle, Purgatory) he sustains his argu-
ments with double references to ancient pagan and
Hebraic-Christian authorities.

The pagan classical and the Hebraic-Christian
religious legacies, marvelously fused from Dante
to Milton, comprehend almost in its entirety the
history of myths, gods, and heroes in Western
culture. There is, however, a third strain in that
history, a strain that develops out of the rationalistic Enlightenment of the 17th and 18th centuries.
After the Renaissance humanists had sought to ignore
their immediate past and link themselves directly
with a revivified pagan antiquity, a battle between
moderns and ancients occurred in which the moderns
sought to wrest themselves free from their classical
as well as their medieval past. On the strength of
reason, they contended, a brave new world could be
articulated, free of antique fables and fairy toys,
whether ancient or medieval. But in the process
of uprooting itself, enlightenment discovered that
it too was a child of history and could not therefore free itself of the past except by knowing
itself to be inextricably rooted in that past.
With that awareness, enlightenment becomes Romantic
or HISTORICAL-MINDED enlightenment. It has given us
in that historical awareness the SENSE of myth,
which is our theme here. When we speak of gods and
heroes and the power of myth in the arts, we take
our content chiefly from the classical and Christian
legacies; but it is romantic enlightenment that provides the critical-historical attitude. In this
sense, the great writers of our age are still
thoroughly romantic, for they must draw on the
classical and Christian legacies of gods and heroes
even when they wish to exorcise them into oblivion.

Critical scholarship distinguishes two levels on
which the power of myth operates. On one level it
is an organizing power. It is excited into being
where there is social chaos. Myth, at such times,
tends to supplant reality in the profoundest depths
of conscience, until reality itself approximates
the shape of myth. On its other level, myth-making
is a disorganizing power. When reality has hardened
or stiffened in its acquired shape, art then

becomes--stage by stage--an expression of disorganizing force. Some call these contrary powers the
Apollonian and Dionysian inspirations, in which
tragedy has its birth. For those who are familiar
with the profound analyses of Hegel on the subject,
those powers animate the epic and lyric voice of
poetry: the one, objective in its imaginative force,
shaping an entire universe and peopling it with gods
and heroes enough to keep it running, while the
common masses gradually learn how to WILL to be free
men and women; the other subjective, expressing the
maturity of such men and women who, in their own
voices and deeds, vie with epic heroes and prepare
the way for tragedy, where lyric subjectivity and
epic objectivity come on stage together.

In his Iliad and Odyssey Homer of course gives us
the organizing myths par excellence; Hesiod, with
his Theogony and Works and Days, prepares us for
the subjective self-assertion of the lyric poets,
and for the grand synthesis of tragedy, by recount-
ing the origins of the gods from a less than heroic
perspective.

For the critical scholar it is in the context of
theogony that the Christian-Hebraic legacy is fused
with the pagan. The Hebraic God of Abraham, Isaac,
and Jacob, through the Pauline preaching of Christ,
brings on a final overthrow of all generations of
the pagan divinities. Critical enlightenment sub-
sequently envisions for its own time the overthrow
and death even of that divine conqueror of the
Olympians, with his hosts of saints and angels, and
all the soaring temples built to his greater glory.
But romantic enlightenment becomes itself LYRICAL
in its iconoclasm; and art therefore survives, myth-
making revives, a new chaos is given shape.

In the time that remains I would like to illustrate in literary terms some of these large defini-
tions and meanings: the fabulous living legacy of
Homer, the chronicle of the rise and fall of the
gods and heroes from Hesiod to Goethe and beyond,
into the lower depths and chaos of today's imaginative wasteland, where myth in literature and film
has so much organizing work to do.

St. Augustine tells us that the learned Varro,
writing of the ancient gods, distinguished three
kinds of "reasoning about gods" or theology: the
MYTHICAL, the PHYSICAL, and the CIVIL. The

mythical--or fabulous--kind, says Varro, is the one
poets prefer. It contains, he says, much in it that
is false, base, and unworthy of the immortal gods,
and it is therefore to be set apart from the
physical or scientific and civil accounts of the
gods. But Augustine goes on to show that, in fact,
it was precisely poets--Homer and Hesiod in
particular--who gave the Greeks their most abiding
accounts of the divinities, so that poetic MYTH is
the sum and substance of their theology, even in
the form in which the Romans took it up. Still,
learned pagans had tried to separate the mythical
from the physical and civil theology--as Varro had
suggested doing--without great determination,
however. Augustine scolds those pagans for shying
away from the truly historical and rational approach
of Euhémerus, who in the fourth century B.C. had
sought to show

> by investigating their actions and recording
> the places of their births and burials, that
> the mythological deities were mere mortal men,
> raised to the rank of gods on account of the
> benefits which they had conferred upon man-
> kind. (Harper's Dictionary)

Those who erected a statue to Jupiter's wet nurse
in the Capitol, St. Augustine goes on to say, were
in fact supporting the view of Euhémerus who "not
with the garrulity of a fable teller but with the
diligence of a historian, maintained that all these
gods had once been mortal men."
    The point Augustine insists on here and through
his long chapters on the subject in The City of God
is that none of the more thoughtful Greeks or Romans
ever took the antique fables or myths of their gods
seriously as a religion. Even in antiquity, in
other words, Western man had a sense that true
religion was something that came to him--if it
came at all--not from his native lands but from
lands to the East. Certainly all serious scholarship and current tendencies and fads since
Augustine's time confirm that view.
    The Greeks had a sort of religion of their own,
of course, the substance of which they inherited,
as they inherited the rudiments of their entire
culture, from Oriental peoples. But they did with

that religion what they did with everything else
they touched: they humanized it, secularized it,
thought it through in all its details. They gave
their inherited gods a history and made that history
a part of their own spiritual evolution.

As the inherited gods of Greece came out of
nature, and as nature had come out of an original
chaos, so the peoples of Greece with their heroes,
institutions, customs, arts, and sciences, evolved
from the gods. But the ultimate phase of that
evolution, the glorious civilization of the Greek
city-states, far surpassed in excellence any and
all the powers, mythical or physical, that contrib-
uted to its formation. Having performed their
genealogical evolutionary function, those powers
would surely have sunk back into original chaos and
oblivion had not the poets and artists of Greece
given them some semblance of immortality, as much
immortality as human imagination has power to give
to airy nothings, by making them fabulous embodiments of idealized humanity to grace the city of
man.

"Homer and Hesiod," wrote Herodotus, "fashioned
our gods for us." He did not mean that they had
"made up" the gods; he respected the accounts of
oriental origins. What he meant was that the poets
had represented the substance of those gods so
completely that long before the time of Phidias
they had become the object not of religious but of
artistic worship. A total absorption of religion
into art, St. Augustine reminds us, characterizes
the FABULOUS and the MYTHICAL. The transcendent
divinity of the Judaic-Christian experience is quite
another thing.

In Homer's world, art's absorption of religion is
already complete. Zeus reigns, with his Olympian
divinities of spirit, truth, and beauty. The
natural divinities still have a PRESENCE: their
force is felt, but it is not a DECISIVE force. They
work darkly, through furies, nemesis, justice, fate.
Poetry prefers the Olympians. Yet we know that
with the inevitable triumph of the prose of reason,
nemesis, the furies, justice, and fate will all
return, as abstract concepts, to dominate the de-
mythologized thought of the West for millenia.

In Homer's Iliad we have gods pulling strings
with heroes as puppets. Or so it appears on the

surface. Closer scrutiny reveals, however, that the divine puppet-masters are really inseparably linked to their puppets. The gods have no serious business beyond pulling the strings of Agamemnon, Achilles, Hector, and the other epic heroes. Thus, from a certain perspective, it is possible to view the puppet-masters themselves as puppets responding to the willful tugs of the heroes below. The secret charm of Homer lies precisely in this paradox: the puppet-equality of gods and heroes. It is this that sets Homer's world "beyond good and evil" in a sense much older than that of Friedrich Nietzsche's use of the term. His gods and heroes are to be marvelled at, not JUDGED. And in marvelling at them we gain an indispensable insight into the meaning of freedom. We learn to see that there is a world of difference between a puppet who knows he is a puppet and one who does NOT know it. A puppet who knows he is a puppet is made free by the truth of such knowledge; a puppet who does NOT know he is a puppet is a captive fool in his ignorance. As Spinoza tells it: FREEDOM IS INSIGHT INTO NECESSITY. In this respect Homer's heroes have an advantage over his gods, for they know (much better than the gods do) that they are puppets. Their spiritual awareness, writes Hegel,

> is higher than that of the gods themselves, for they are ACTUALLY what the gods are IMPLICITLY. They represent the carrying into effect of what is implicit, and if they have also to struggle and work, this is a "working off" of the natural element which the gods still have in themselves. The gods come out of the powers of nature; the heroes come out of the gods.

Beyond the puppet-scene of gods and heroes, in other words, is fate, destiny, necessity. Zeus knows this. That's why he doesn't take his sovereignty over the other gods too seriously. But the heroes' consciousness of fate and necessity is even clearer. They know it as the HEGEMONY of NEMESIS, that incomprehensible power that brings down the exalted and the mighty and establishes equality.

According to Hegel the spiritual history of the Greeks, in the sphere of conduct, consists precisely

in an ever-deepening insight into this necessity or
fate. At first, it is perceived as blind, or
rather, as a dark spot above the world of Homer,
the presence of which betrays the Olympian gods.
The Greeks who loved their Homer saw that his gods
and heroes were really one, that the gods were in
fact the PASSIONS of the heroes objectified as
necessity. Hegel comments, "The Greek who has
within him the feeling of that necessity calms his
soul with it." It prompts him to say "It is so;
there is nothing to be done about it." As Albert
Camus stresses in his Myth of Sisyphus, the power
of the Greek myths, understood in this way, is a
liberating organizing force.

T. S. Eliot makes this point in an early review
of Joyce's Ulysses titled "Ulysses, Order and Myth,"
which appeared in The Dial in 1923. Eliot insists
that Joyce's use of Homer was by no means an
"amusing dodge." On the contrary, the "mythical
method" (as he calls it) is a technique that makes
it possible for the modern writer to make sense out
of the seemingly blind, meaningless necessities of
modern existence. "Manipulating a continuous
parallel between contemporaneity and antiquity,"
Eliot wrote, helps make the "modern world possible
for art."

Eliot himself, as we know, made use of Greek
mythology in a very obvious way in many of his
works. Edmund Wilson, who gives a chapter each to
Eliot and Joyce in Axel's Castle, has high praise
for such use of myth, which has nothing of the
antiquarian in it. But he warns also that

> this tendency to look to the past, in spite
> of the revolutionary character of some of
> their methods, has sometimes given even to
> their most original work an odd Alexandrian
> aspect: the productions of Eliot, Proust,
> and Joyce, for example, are sometimes veri-
> table literary museums. It is not merely
> that these modern novelists and poets build
> upon their predecessors, as the greatest
> writers have done in all times, but that they
> have developed a weakness for recapitulating
> them in parodies.

To parody the Homeric myths, while using them to organize an otherwise chaotic experience, is to recapitulate what happened in the age of Hesiod. Hesiod debunks the Homeric heroes. For him, they are "gift-devouring princes" who gloat in their heroic irresponsibility even as hawks gloat over the nightingales on which they prey. But their loss is common humanity's gain. Hesiod, moreover, with keener insight, takes the gold out of Homer's golden age by translating blind fate or necessity into a retributive power.

Unlike Homer's heroes, who are beyond good and evil, Hesiod's common men and less-than-heroic lords have an instinctive sense that our fate is EARNED through human actions. The curse on the house of Agamemnon is hinted at in the Odyssey; but Hesiod spells it out. What seems to go wrong in the world, by chance, is indeed something fated (about which we can do nothing), but fated through the willful actions of men. Objective fate becomes a subjective prompting, something willed from within. And that, Hegel reminds us, marks the psychological transition from epic to lyric poetry.

By way of Hesiod we move from Homer's objective narrative to the subjective songs of Sappho and Anacreon and their peers. The Greek lyric poets cease to look up to Homer's heroes because they have raised themselves to be, subjectively, pretty much the same thing. Sappho, in her dealings with her one true god, Aphrodite, takes an heroic attitude, fully conscious that her foam-borne divinity is her very own spirit, objectified. Anacreon says it in the plainest terms. When Eros attacks him from outside, to make him fall in love, he can defend himself; but when he realizes that the struggle is really inside him, within his own subjective awareness, all efforts at defending himself are vain and useless. The puppet strings have disappeared.

With lyric subjectivity, or self-awareness, the "unstrung" heroes are ready to fret and strut their hour upon the stage as "persons" of the drama. On stage, Homer's blind fate, Hesiod's retributive necessity, the lyric poets' subjective willfulness (felt as the god within) become JUST JUDGMENT. This insight into necessity is perfected, in Greek tragedy, as the liberating force which can make ALL men

free and equal. And that glorious moment of myth,
when the heroic is brought down to earth, the divine
and human combined through a cathartic experience
which allows both heroes and commoners to say IT IS
SO, marks the culmination and end of the Greek
experience. Homer's heroes were beyond good and
evil; Hesiod's vision traced a retributive nemesis
which leveled heroes and raised commoners almost
indiscriminately; Greek tragedy defines, for the
first time in history, a discriminating justice
which--even in tragic reversals that seem ironic--
emerges as EQUITY. Beyond such justice is PROV-
IDENCE. But that is beyond Greek experience, which
must here give way to that of the Jews and the
Romans.

The Aeneid, no less than the OLD TESTAMENT, shows
us the workings of providence. Providential God
works toward fixed ends and, through those he
chooses, his ends are realized. Those whom he makes
willing to be chosen become his pious heroes. For
them, IT IS SO becomes SO BE IT. God's providence
has its way with the unwilling too, of course. But
that is graceless. Subjective piety makes possible
a graceful obedience through virtual identity with
the objective will of God. Consummation of that
identity, which results in a new freedom as much
divine as human, is achieved, many say, in the
grandest and greatest of all tragedies; the man-God
or God-man protagonist there proves in tragic death
that what dies in him is death itself. In his
"Dialogue on Dramatic Poetry" (1928), Eliot suggests
that the "consummation of drama, the perfect and
ideal drama, is to be found in the ceremony of the
Mass." He concludes with a rhetorical question:
"When drama has ranged as far as it has in our own
day, is not the only solution to return to religious
liturgy?"

"Credo quia absurdum," Tertullian said of that
crucifixion-tragedy of tragedies. And whether we
believe that colossal absurdity or not, the fact is
that the myths of Greece and Rome could no longer
serve as an organizing force in this context. Art
thereafter looks toward spaceless eternity with
Christian piety which is also contempt for the
world. For centuries the monastic saintly call to
renounce the world will prevail; not until all the
world, including the Germanic peoples, has answered

that call and entered the Church do we find a return
to the organizing insights of the ancient legacy.

Dante belongs to the time of that return. For
him, as for us today, art, perhaps more than religion, was a redemption of the absurd. His Church
seemed ready to burst at the seams with its worldly
cares and concerns--politics, economics, culture,
all of which (though perfectly NATURAL) were pre-
empting the claims of grace. There had to be a
separation, giving nature its due and freeing grace.
Like so many of his age, Dante resists the separation, finds it too painful from a humanistic point
of view, though he understands the necessity for
it. It is not surprising, therefore, to find in
the _Divine Comedy_ that the pagan gods are called
falsi e bugiardi--even though Virgil (the Homeric
Virgil) is at Dante's side. Virgil's presence is
no accident of course; Dante draws on it to prime
himself, and us, for a reversal of the poetic
course so far outlined, from Homer to the New
Testament. Under his providential God, Dante parallels in reverse the experience of Virgil's
Aeneas--just as Milton, with his divine nemesis
that casts out rebellion from heaven and disobe-
dience from Eden, will later parallel Hesiod.

Between Dante and Milton, Shakespeare holds a
place corresponding to that of the Greek tragedians
between Hesiod and Virgil.

Needless to say, with my broad outlines, I have
been reciting in haste the creed of our modern
romantic theogony, which traces the power and
history of the older heroes and myths through a
vast curve from Homer to Hesiod and the lyric poets
of Greece, then on through the Greek tragedians and
Virgil to the Old Testament of the Jews and the New
Testament of Christianity. From there, in a reverse
pattern, through Dante, Shakespearean tragedy, and
Miltonic theogonies, we get to Goethe's _Faust_, where
we are again--as in Homer--beyond good and evil yet
poles removed from Homeric innocence. We are back
to blind fate, that dark spot over Homer's golden
world, now viewed as the dreadful existential wasteland of James Thomson, Sartre, T. S. Eliot, Pound,
and all who come after them down that line.

That, briefly, is the pattern of the divine dialectic, or battle of the gods, by which the divinities and truths of one age become the fables and

falsehoods of another. It shapes the history of philosophy, science, and social thought--from Plato and Aristotle to Darwin, Marx, Nietzsche, and Freud --no less than it does the literary history of Western mythology. Hesiod, as we noted, is the poet who first brought this pattern of struggle or dialectic into literary focus to illustrate the workings of nemesis. His Theogony--that "most ancient monument that we have of the Greek mythology"--does indeed exhibit, as Harry Thurston Peck long ago observed, the "mixture of meanness and grandeur which characterizes a strong but un-cultivated genius." Yet, he hastened to add that the "passage relating to the battle of the gods, together with the combat of Zeus and Typhoeus, as-tonishes the reader by sudden bursts of enthusiasm." Touching on the Miltonic parallel which we draw, Professor Peck noted that the "arming of the Messiah for the battle in Paradise Lost is obvi-ously imitated from the magnificent picture of Zeus summoning all the terrors of his omnipotence for the extirpation of the Titans."

The first great battle of the gods brought down the spacious sky's natural divinities. Cronos, time, triumphs over Uranus. In modern terms Cronos is the force of permanent revolution. What can resist the overturning power of time, the dialec-tical force of history? The story of Time's over-throw by Zeus is the Greek answer. Zeus and Mnemosyne--memory--give birth to the nine muses who celebrate in every variety of poetry, dance, music, history, and science the triumph of spiritual force over space and time. Beauty, which is for the spirit what claps of thunder and bolts of lightning are in the natural world, arrests time, stops it dead in its tracks. For beauty's sake, Homer tells us, the Trojan war was fought and justified. And when Greece gave itself to the loving pursuit of truth, it equated beauty with it, for it could only love the BEAUTIFUL. When the Greek city-state civilization fell, the beauty of its philosophic thought as well as its art so fascinated its con-querors that, so far as they could, they made them-selves Greek. The Romans made Greek mythology their own. And not until that mythology had lost its organizing power (even when sustained by large government subsidies) did the practical Romans, late in imperial times, consent to its overthrow as the official Roman worship.

The history of Roman political institutions, it is worth noting, became in time a myth in its own right, precisely because of the tremendous organizing power contained in it. The history of the mythical fascination exerted by Roman governmental institutions and public law--particularly its effect on Dante--is documented in a fine book called _Dante and the Myth of Rome_. The Romans no doubt felt animated by the power of poetic myth in making history, and that must be why so many who later studied Roman history invariably recognized the power of myth in it.

In "The Truest Daughter of Dido: Racine's _Berenice_," Martin Mueller observes how, in the early Renaissance, humanists like Trissino--who sought to restore Attic tragedy--did not turn to the Greeks for themes and certainly not to mythology for their protagonists. "Trissino's _Sofonisba_, the first European tragedy to aim self-consciously at a restoration of Attic tragedy," writes Mueller,

> is a displaced Dido tragedy. Trissino's choice of subject reveals a sophisticated degree of reflection on the problematical nature of imitation. Whereas with regard to form he aimed at a faithful reproduction of the dramatic conventions of Attic tragedy, with regard to subject matter he was intent on reproducing the relationship between audience and stage characters that obtained in his models. He saw the 'equivalent' of Greek myth in Roman history. What Medea and Phaedra had signified in the drama of fifth-century Athens, Sofonisba was to signify for the new tragedy of sixteenth-century Italy.

But, for reasons suggested earlier, the humanistic effort to resurrect the classical past failed, giving way to a rationalist enlightenment that sought to spin out of itself, like a spider, a model world. The enlightenment's contribution to the history of the battles of the gods is perhaps best suggested by the story in Rabelais' account of the education of Pantagruel. Rabelais there tells

us of the effect on that marvelous boy of the reading of Plutarch's account of the proclamation of
the death of the great god Pan, in the reign of
Tiberius Caesar. The story of Pan's end was so
touchingly told, writes Rabelais, that it brought
tears as large as ostrich eggs rolling from the
eyes of Pantagruel, who mistakenly referred it to

> our Lord and Savior, Jesus Christ, "ignomin-
> iously put to death by the envy and iniquity
> of the pontiffs, doctors, presbyters, and
> monks of the Mosaic dispensation."

In a satire entitled "Great Christ is Dead," James
Thomson (the same we quoted earlier) tells the
Rabelaisian story as prelude to a brilliant survey
of the literature of the passing of the gods since
the time of Rabelais. That passing, which saw
nature annulled and supernature enthroned, has
indeed been a favorite theme of great writers, who,
according to their religion, fantasy, and mood,
have variously celebrated it in song (to say
nothing of novels and films). Milton in his hymn
to the Nativity of Christ shouted harsh puritanical
scorn upon the "oracles stricken dumb and the
deities overthrown." Shelley in "Hellas" does not
contest the justice of the doom of pagan divinities
with their heroes, but he predicts the same doom for
their Galilean conqueror, in his turn. Swinburne
bewailed the vanquished pagan immortals "with
nothing but aversion and contempt for the pale
Galilean." Leopardi in an early poem regrets the
loss of the ancient divinities and appeals "to
Nature to restore to his spirit its first fire, if
indeed she lives." Schiller passionately laments
them in his "Gods of Greece," and Mrs. Browning has
no less passionately answered him. Novalis also
laments the unsouling of nature, as he says, but
"goes on to celebrate the resurrection of humanity
in Christ." But James Thomson's favorite on the
theme of the passing of the ancient gods is Heinrich
Heine, who certainly merits a distinguished place in
any serious treatment of the theme OLD GODS/NEW
HEROES.
    Heine gives us a wild picture of the Olympian
gods "holding high revelry, with nectar and ambrose,
with Apollonian music and inextinguishable

laughter." Suddenly there is an unexpected commotion. The doors are blown open and

> a wretched Jew staggers in, his brow bleeding
> from a crown of thorns, trailing on his
> shoulder a heavy cross, which he heaves upon
> the banquet table; and forthwith the revel is
> no more, the divine feast disappears, the
> everburning lights are quenched, the trium-
> phant gods and goddesses vanish terror-
> stricken, dethroned for ever and ever.

Heine in his "Gods of Greece" says that he has
never really loved the old deities, that to him the
Greeks generally were repugnant and the Romans
"thoroughly hateful." Yet, he hastens to add that
when he considers how dastardly and windy are the
gods and heroes who overcame them--the "new reigning
sorrowful gods, malignant in their sheep's clothing
of humility"--he feels a powerful urge to fight for
the old against the new. It is in his "Gods in
Exile" that Heine pictures for us what became of
the dispersed Olympians during the Dark Ages

> in the thick night of the noontide of
> Christianity; how they were transformed from
> celestial to infernal by the monstrous super-
> stition of that baleful realm; as we find the
> hoofs and horns of Pan transferred to the
> Devil himself; as we find Venus in that
> legend of Tannhäuser which has fascinated so
> many poets, as well as great Wagner--

> Vénus, ma belle déesse,
> Vous êtes diablesse.

Heine's mood, of course, is a belated experience of
the mood Boccaccio indulged (in a land where such
moods come faster). In the pleasant expectation
that gloomy institutionalized Christianity might
some day be banished from the face of the earth by
hearty laughter, Boccaccio, in his Rabelaisian
phase, compared Christianity to a plague: it was a
plague more infectious and destructive than the
merely physical plague from which the storytellers
of his Decameron flee. It was a SPIRITUAL plague.
In his lovely Ninfale Fiesolano, Boccaccio had

dreamt of a world restored to pristine pagan innocence. If only priests and nuns and monks would
shout from the housetops what they must be saying
in their hearts, the thick cloud of medieval gloom
would be lifted!

But in the 19th century what was happening under
the romantic struggle of which Heine is an expression was an awakening, as we said, of the historical
sense that looked for reason not in the abstract--
not reason as an OUGHT TO BE to be applied in judgment AGAINST history--but reason in history itself.

The idea of searching out reason in history, as
it has actually been, the way astronomers for
example seek out reason in the actual motions of
the heavenly bodies, not in some abstract astro-
nomical OUGHT TO BE that never was, is the basis
of all our serious modern culture.

Who in literature today does not live on the
power of myth? Film, which lays lines and colors
only temporarily on a white screen, is so obviously
such stuff as dreams are made on that there is no
doubting its myth-making character. The film does
indeed give to airy nothing, in Shakespeare's
sense, a local habitation and a name, giving joy in
a way that can be "in widest commonality spread,"
as the phrase goes. The myth-making power of film
covers a wide spectrum, from the John Wayne/Clint
Eastwood versions of latter-day heroes to the more
subtle kind of myth-making--at once historical and
original, old and new, familiar and distracting--
which is to be found in such top masters of film
myths as Alain Resnais, Ingmar Bergman, and Federico
Fellini. Fellini, and in a more obvious but perhaps
less varied and less marvelous way, Antonioni, have
shown us the far-reaching potential of film as the
contemporary myth-maker. There are always five
minutes at least in every Antonioni film which are
nothing more than a focusing, a zooming in of the
camera on a number of very ordinary-looking objects,
empty rooms, prosaic routines. The build-up is
excruciating in a double sense; its significance is
not all clear at the outset, and it may seem much
too long a sequence--in many cases--for what is
stated. Still, that lingering commentary of the
camera makes possible the sort of vibrant statement
that externalizes the inward or subjective language
of personality in an objective manner which does not

work objectively on stage, for instance. Antonioni
gives us in its stark expression the new language
of myth-exhaustion--a language which Fellini employs
to express the positive residue of that cultural
exhaustion. Old familiar myths are restructured in
Fellini's context--loss of innocence; dark nights
of orgiastic terror; the new dawn which always
brings sorrow, guilt, and the realization of eternal
separation; Orphic descents into hell; Dantesque and
biblical overtones sharply rendered and often
reinforced through familiar color symbolism--in an
existential setting made articulate and immediately
relevant through the unique idiom of film.
Antonioni and Fellini have created, through their
innovative film techniques, a new medium for the
expression of contemporary myths in an existential
world. Fellini, in particular, has shown the
extraordinary possibilities for recreating and
commenting on familiar myths in contemporary terms,
and if others have fallen behind, the direction for
the future nonetheless has been mapped out.

It is easier and perhaps in the long run more
rewarding from a literary point of view to examine
the modern techniques of myth-building and myth-
making as it has been developed on stage, in
dramatic art. And in a way, theater--with its local
habitation for living players--is still the creative
center for myth-making, as it early became for the
Greeks. Two names, one recent, the other contemporary, deserve to be mentioned here: Pirandello
and Edward Albee. In my opinion they are the most
exciting and original playwrights and myth-makers
of our age. Pirandello's marvelously MYTHICAL mind
is evident in all his works, but especially in the
last plays, where he focuses on the myth-making
which is art (The Mountain Giants), religion
(Lazarus), and politics (The New Colony). There is
a genial passage in Pirandello's novel Il fu Mattia
Pascal where one of the characters speaks of the
transition from Orestes to Hamlet--and I have used
and explicated the suggestions of that passage in
my book on Pirandello. Here I would like to recall
the passage very briefly because it sums up beautifully much of what I have already said and because
it is itself infinitely suggestive. Pirandello--
through his character--asks us to picture a puppet-
show Orestes with his sword drawn, about to avenge

his father's murder. Suddenly a hole is ripped in
the paper sky of the puppet theater, and down
through that hole come all sorts of new (or unknown-
to-the Greeks) things. The audience is irresistibly
drawn to look up, to see what is coming down,
filtering through that hole. Orestes too looks up.
What happens then, Pirandello's spokesman says, is
exactly what happens in Hamlet. And that, he concludes, is the difference between the ancient and
the modern theater--a hole in the paper sky . . .
through which distracting new things come down upon
us.

That Pirandellian mythic interpretation of the
metamorphosis of the classical into modern drama
should remind us that Hamlet himself was the first
to "dramatize" the transformation. In shattering
the old gods he adheres to his own almost
Pirandellian conscience. Particularly in his use
of a play within his own play, to penetrate an
opaque reality, Hamlet illustrates the modern
instinct for self-confrontation.

In the last great phase of his dramatic productivity, Pirandello turned--as I have indicated--
quite literally to myth-making. But even before
that last and still-to-be-properly-assessed period
in his life as a playwright, in the theater plays
and Henry IV, for example, he shatters the old gods
of convention through that ironic paradox which is
also the base and sustenance of classical tragedy.

Edward Albee, too, uses art for redemption of
the absurd. Like Pirandello he preserves--
paradoxically--what he rejects. Albee, of course,
is representative in a sense of a whole school of
contemporary dramatic myth-makers, and in any
anthology he must be placed under the general rubric
"Theater of the Absurd." And yet even in his
earliest plays he reveals something unique and quite
different from such playwrights as Anouilh,
Giradoux, and Sartre. Albee does not play on the
obvious classical myths. But he does use what
Thomson called "antique fables" with a vengeance.
His early The Zoo Story is a modern crucifixion and
an ironic brand of self-sacrifice, seen and drama-
tized, as it were, through a glass darkly. There
are myths within myths, fables within fables, in
the fertile Son-Father-Immaculate Conception
suggestion of Who's Afraid of Virginia Woolf?--with

its mass for the dead and the exhaustion of hope at the end of that play. There is an ingenious negative Dantesque allegory--a parody on a high level--running through that powerful and perhaps not-fully-understood masterpiece of his, Tiny Alice. There is fable and myth of a different kind in the evolutionary commentary translated into human behavior in his most recent play, Seascape, where history is reduced to a simple equation of fossilized spiritual meanings, stiffened molds of human conduct, and where the sensitive lizards of Ooze--very like some ancient heroes swimming into our ken--break those molds, leaving behind a question and a confusion which already contains a kind of answer.

Perhaps because he is not imitating so much as using old fables and fairy toys Albee can be surprisingly effective. He is by far the most ingenious of our contemporary myth-makers. I should mention at least one of his most interesting dramatic devices, because it enables us to grasp intuitively at least--the way all good drama enables us to do--the spiraling of myth on myth, the dialectic of paradoxical dramatic structures, the juxtaposition of old and new. In almost all his plays Albee interrupts the action at the most crucial point to tell a story--symbolic dogs who are real enough to bite; cats who turn suddenly from affectionate response to indifference and finally hatred of their masters; a zoo which is a circus of the beasts in all of us and also a very familiar place and the world which is made up of such circuses; stories of dreams of madness and hallucinations of sanctity, imaginary sons who kill imaginary parents and are killed in turn by those who, in their weakness, created such idle yet monstrous heroes. Albee's stories are modern allegorical fables as effective, in their way, as any ballads of troubadors or Homeric tales.

"To create, today," Albert Camus says in The Rebel, "is to create dangerously." That too is perhaps a myth, for myths lurk all around us.

2

ON THE LITERARY USE OF MYTH

William C. Johnson, Jr.

To investigate myth in literature is, nowadays,
almost surely to encounter the hydra, Chaos. The
term <u>myth</u> has endured chimaeric transformations at
the hands of various linguistic and philosophical
schools of thought. The presence of myth in literature, moreover, raises epistemological, even ontological questions, for if it is true that mythic
narratives are in important ways nonliterary, the
question arises as to how these radically different
modes of discourse can come together. It may be,
as C. S. Lewis argued, that "the value of myth is
not a specifically literary value, nor the appreciation of myth a specifically literary experience."[1]
Here I shall focus initially on one aspect of myth
in order to provide a basis for some observations
on how myths are used in literary works.

An aspect of myth often overlooked amidst the
current emphasis on abstract models is the presentation of the sacred. This essentially religious
function is often subsumed in more particularistic
methods of analysis. Mircea Eliade has stressed the
sacred function in several of his books. In his
words,

> myths describe the various and sometimes
> dramatic breakthroughs of the sacred (or the

24

'supernatural') into the World. It is this
sudden breakthrough of the sacred that really
establishes the World and makes it what it is
today.[2]

Eliade's emphasis finds expression in other disciplines by scholars such as Jung, Frankfort,
Coomarswamy, and Joseph Campbell.[3] In this context,
myths are viewed as essentially validatory: they
remind a culture of the sacred origins and nature of
the object or institution in question. Although
this view does not explain all myths, it offers
significant possibilities that modern literature
has only minimally explored.

Our own historical situation, furthermore, is the
result of a process through which myths have become
secularized and have therefore lost their original
sacrality. Many terms have been coined for this
process, such as Eliade's "de-sacralization" and
"de-mythicization," Jung's "withdrawal of projections," Owen Barfield's "internalization," or C. S.
Lewis's more inclusive phrase, "the psychological
history of the West."[4] The fact remains, however,
that once western societies drift into a "Renaissance" condition identifying with self, time,
history, individualism, empiricism, and so on, then
several things happen to the sacred elements of
myths: they are forgotten or ignored; they are used
for new secular purposes; or they are perpetuated
in underground or "off-beat" cultural forms, often
in what Eliade calls "degraded" forms.[5]

Not surprisingly, the same forces that secularize
myth generate literature. An interest in man and
his experience for its own sake creates new modes
of discourse. The initiatory quest of myth, for
example, becomes the psychological journey of self-
discovery in literature. Two literary uses of myth
concern me here; these I shall call Participation
and Appropriation. The first refers to the effort
to perpetuate in literature the original sacred
function of a symbol or practice, the second to the
use of myth for ulterior purposes moving away from
sacred and into secular experience.

The second alternative, Appropriation, is today
the more familiar approach to myth. Yeats's use of
Celtic lore, Eliot's use of the Grail legend, and
Joyce's use of Homer provide well-known illustra-

tions.   There may be sacred overtones in such works,
but they do not partake of an underlying system of
sacred meanings.   Douglas Bush's comments on English
Romantic and Victorian uses of myth would apply also
to many contemporary writers:

> Poets, more or less alienated from accepted
> religious, political and social creeds and
> attitudes, reinterpreted myths predominantly
> as vehicles for their own experience or
> vision or their own reflections on the prob-
> lems of their age.[7]

While mythic character, situations, and symbols
often appear in modern literature, they usually
express not the sacred but idiosyncratic private
experience.   Nonetheless, myths and mythic symbols
do survive.   A sharper distinction between Participative or sacred use and Appropriative or humanistic
use can facilitate our current understanding of
possibilities for the use of myth in literature.
   Some will object to a sharp distinction between
sacred and secular uses of myth.   Such objections,
however, usually arise from literary preferences
for certain forms and styles, preferences often
based on an implicit humanism, which is offended at
being excluded from the possibility of the sacred.
Literary expectations of this sort, however, do not
always apply to our experience of mythic narratives.
The presence of the permanent, the fantastic, and
the numinous that we sense in reading the myths of,
say, Demeter or Ragnarok may reoccur as a "mythic
quality" in works of literature, but it affects
us not because of the author's verbal technique but
because it expresses, as Lewis suggests, a "value
independent of its embodiment in any literary work"
(p. 41).   A myth, Lewis continues, "is felt to be
inevitable.   And the first hearing is chiefly valu-
able in introducing us to a permanent object of
contemplation--more like a thing than a narration"
(p. 43).   Sensitive and talented writers have, of
course, applied themselves to the articulation of
myths--Thoreau's Walden providing the classic
American example.   Such moments, however, have been
rare in western literary history, so that Lewis's
argument remains essentially sound.   It remains
worthwhile, even so, to illustrate further the

differences between participative and appropriative
uses of myth.

For examples I turn to popular fiction of the
turn of the century. The appeal of ghost stories
to people of this period is not surprising, given
the rationalistic bent of the late Victorian age.
Henry James, H. P. Lovecraft, and Kipling, for
example, often make use of the supernatural in their
fiction. For purposes of contrast I have chosen
stories by two lesser known writers. M. R. James's
"The Ash Tree" and Algernon Blackwood's "The Man
Whom the Trees Loved" have in common the use of
trees as unifying supernatural symbols but differ
distinctively in their approaches.

The tree itself, of course, is a widespread
ancient mythic symbol appearing in various forms,
such as the architectural pillar, the ladder to
heaven, the cross, the totem pole, and the human
body. Such forms are ultimately homological variations of the _axis mundi_ or world tree, perhaps best
known to the western world for its role in Norse
mythology. In primitive mythologies the tree expresses the _power_ of the living cosmos endlessly
renewing itself. The many tales of divinities
dwelling in trees, of trees giving birth to men,
and of trees as repositories of ancestral souls,
reveal the generative qualities of this power.[8]
That a tree is mysteriously powerful is, likewise,
at the heart of both tales here chosen for illustration.

"The Ash Tree" is typical of many Gothic tales.
It can be summarized as follows:

> In the late seventeenth century, the proprie-
> tor of an English estate witnesses a woman
> gathering sprigs from an ash tree near his
> house. He accuses her of witchcraft and she
> is tried and executed. Later, the proprietor
> and a descendant both suffer mysterious and
> horrible deaths while sleeping in a room next
> to the tree. It is finally discovered that
> the woman has risen from the grave, inhabited
> the tree, and sent forth poisonous, vampire-
> like spiders to climb up the tree into the
> bedroom and murder their prey.

James's literary approach reveals a psychological appropriation of the supernatural. Through the ignorance of his characters as to the cause of the murders, the hints of witchcraft, and an urbane and politely skeptical narrator, James communicates horror by projecting a rational distance from the supernatural. The following passage, in which two gentlemen decide to investigate the tree, is representative:

> "There is something more than we know of in that tree, my lord. I am for an instant search."
> And this was agreed upon. A ladder was brought, and one of the gardeners went up, and, looking down the hollow, could detect nothing but a few dim indications of something moving. They got a lantern, and let it down by a rope.
> "We must get at the bottom of this. My life upon it, my lord, but the secret of these terrible deaths is there."[9]

The supernatural here is an emotional stimulus, at first unknown, which is eventually discovered with horrific surprise, penetrated, and finally destroyed in the burning of the tree. As the unifying symbol of the story, the tree represents emotional terror, its destruction a return to rational normality. The tree functions humanistically as an instrument to reveal human terror and as such is decidedly unlike the sacred trees of mythology, which reveal the supernatural power of the cosmos. Here we do not participate in the supernatural but rather view it from the other side of a protective shield erected by human reason. In a word, James writes from the popular Victorian viewpoint of implicit disbelief. Symbolic potentialities of the tree are expressed as human reactions to the tree's horrific function.

This tale is not in every respect typical of the literary appropriation of myth. Gothic horror is not representative of modern literature. Nonetheless, it is representative, in a subtle way, of a prevalent modern attitude toward myths. An archaic supernatural symbol is used to stimulate private emotional experience. Supernaturalism is appropriated by emotional aestheticism. The same could be

said of the subtler and literarily more sophisti-
cated applications of supernatural mystery of Henry
James in The Turn of the Screw or "The Jolly
Corner."

Blackwood's approach to the same symbol differs
distinctly. "The Man Whom the Trees Loved" can be
summarized as follows:

> A retired civil servant living on the edge of
> a forest in Hampshire, David Bittacy has been
> fascinated by trees all his life. While
> lodging with Bittacy and his wife, a young
> artist sharpens Bittacy's awareness of this
> feeling. Bittacy's gradual recognition of
> the forest's sway over his imagination coin-
> cides with the approach of the forest itself,
> which seeks out the man who loves it. Despite
> the terrified resistance of his wife, Bittacy
> finally disappears, absorbed into the forest.

The tale reveals not the horror of an unnatural
deformity but the sacred power of nature itself. In
Blackwood's treatment, nature and supernature inter-
penetrate in a symbolic situation suggestive of the
greatest myths. The solitary cedar in Bittacy's
yard, for example, is a sentinel, protecting the
couple from the surge of the forest--a kind of
shamanistic guardian or talismanic figure. When the
tree is blown down, Bittacy cannot resist the call
of the forest, and his house is gradually surrounded
by tree spirits. The cedar functions simultaneously
as a mysterious boundary and as a link between man
and the numinous depth of nature.

Blackwood similarly anticipates rationalistic
appropriation of the supernatural. He achieves this
through his characterization of Bittacy's wife, who
belongs to the daylight world of Protestant ration-
alism and clings firmly to a literal interpretation
of experience. Yet the forest penetrates even her
stubborn defenses:

> His fate! The darkness of some vague, enor-
> mous terror dropped its shadow on her when
> she thought of it. Some instinct in her heart
> she dreaded infinitely more than death--for
> death meant sweet translation for his soul--
> came gradually to associate the thought of him

> with the thought of trees, in particular with
> these Forest trees. Sometimes, before she
> could face the thing, argue it away, or pray
> it into silence, she found the thought of him
> running swiftly through her mind like a
> thought of the Forest itself, the two most
> intimately linked and joined together, each a
> part and complement of the other, one being.[10]

In this mingling of mental and "environmental" in-
fluences, the spirit of the forest is at once
natural and human. Blackwood places his characters,
to borrow again from Eliade, in a "boundary situation," in which man is defined by both the inward-
ness and the otherness of the supernatural. Similarly, the relationship between the worlds of dream
and waking, of fantasy and logic, of self and not-
self, becomes less distinct, so that the cosmos and
man "participate" each other in the author's "micro/
macrocosmic" tale. The sacrality of the forest
finally transcends simple dichotomies: it is simply
real--an authentic supernatural presence. In contrast to James's appropriative isolation of man
from the supernatural, Blackwood's supernaturalism
is participative, recalling in a modern literary
context the function of mythic narratives that once
revealed the presence of sacred power in the profane
world.

In historical terms myths of course have many
functions--cosmogonic, validatory, etiological,
entertaining, and so on. I have stressed two literary approaches to myth in the hopes of better clarifying its possible uses in the present age. Literature, however, is just one of several touchstones
here. Many contemporary disciplines are coming to
recognize that language itself holds the key to
whatever realities man can apprehend. Blackwood
himself wrote in a preface:

> The Mystical Experience known to many through-
> out the ages with invariable similarity is not
> a pathogenic experience, but is due to a
> desirable, genuine and valuable expansion of
> consciousness which furnishes knowledge
> normally ahead of the race, but since language
> can only describe the experience of the race,
> it is incommunicable because no words exist,

and only those who have experienced it can
comprehend it . . . (p. ix).

Blackwood sensed the dilemma facing the modern
artist who seeks to communicate sacred experience.
How can authentic sacrality be expressed in a language and culture infected by so much misplaced
empiricism, agnosticism, and imaginative stagnation?
Or in an intellectual and academic context, how can
myth be experienced religiously when it is so often
merely studied--as another exercise in reducing
experience to the deceptive neatness of formal
structures?[11] The question of how much one's language can be made to say is relative to both artist
and audience: to imaginative capacity and to world
view.

Such questions are perhaps unanswerable at
present. Blackwood implies, however, that we must
create new meanings, or rather, recapitulate in a
new key ancient ways of thinking. One final illustration centering on language may make more sense
of the paradox of trying to say what seems unsay-
able. Despite its better efforts, modern linguis-
tics has not developed a satisfactory theory of
meaning--the sine qua non of living language.[12]
Another of Blackwood's stories, "Malahide and
Forden," suggests why language cannot be reduced to
a system of abstract formalization. The title
refers to two actors undertaking a psychic journey
toward death. This journey has a literal-geographic
counterpart reported by their traveling companion,
the narrator. As the three walk the interface
between the worlds of life and death, they experience a trans-rational interpenetration of thought,
intention, and expression. The narrator comments:

> There is the literal meaning of the actual
> words; there is the meaning of the sentence
> itself; and there is the meaning, above and
> beyond both these, in which the whole of the
> utterer is concerned, a meaning, that is,
> which the unconscious secret part in him--the
> greater part--tries and hopes to say. This
> last, the most significant of all three, since
> it includes cause as well as result, makes of
> every common sentence a legend and a parable.
> Gesture, tone of voice betray its trend; what

> is omitted, or between the lines, betrays
> still more. Its full meaning, being in
> relation to unknown categories, is usually
> hidden both from utterer and hearers. It
> deals simultaneously with the past, the
> present and--the future (p. 215).

Such knowledge of the "deep structure" of language
is more comprehensive and more forceful than struc-
turalist theory, which constructs deliberately
abstract models by the artificial breaking-down of
the "object" under study. Blackwood's view is
mythic in something of the ancient sense, culti-
vating not objectivity but a qualitative realm of
extra-human relations to which man is yet vitally
related.

If myths continue to be a profound, if often
overlooked, domain of experience, as Blackwood,
Eliade, and others have suggested, then we cannot
limit our study of myths to scientific control of
their empirical features. Joseph Campbell notes
that myths "are not invented but occur, and are
recognized by seers, and poets, to be then culti-
vated and employed as catalysts of spiritual . . .
well being."[13] Because a myth is not an object in
the ordinary sense but rather a subtle system of
relations, we must also experience it personally.
We may be occasionally surprised to find such
experiences affording glimpses of the sacred.
Literary uses of myth, then, call attention to the
central choice facing not only artists but contemporary civilization as a whole.

NOTES

[1]Experiment in Criticism (Cambridge Univ. Press,
1961), p. 46. Subsequent references are to this
edition.

[2]Myth and Reality, tr. W. Trask (New York:
Harper, 1963), p. 6. A definition of the sacred is
beyond the scope of this essay, though initially it
might be said that a thing becomes sacred insofar
as it reveals something numinously other than itself

yet also present in human experience. See Eliade's
Patterns in Comparative Religion, tr. R. Sheed
(New York: World, 1963), pp. 12-14, 30, and Owen
Barfield, Saving the Appearances (New York:
Harcourt, n.d.).

[3]For a thorough survey of approaches to myth,
including an application of Levi-Strauss's "struc-
turalist" effort, see G. S. Kirk, Myth: Its Meaning
and Functions in Ancient and Other Cultures
(Cambridge Univ. Press, 1970).

[4]Lewis's views appear in The Discarded Image
(Cambridge Univ. Press, 1964), pp. 42, 215.

[5]Heinrich Zimmer, The King and the Corpse
(Princeton Univ. Press, 1956), pp. 67-201, inter-
prets Arthurian romances as "camouflaged" myths.

[6]Neither process is, of course, unique to modern
literature. Kirk observes of Greek drama of the
fifth century B.C.: ". . . it was predominantly a
literary creation, quite separate in form, method
and intention either from spontaneous myths of the
pre-literate past or from their transitional
descendants" (p. 250).

[7]Pagan Myth and Christian Tradition in English
Poetry (Philadelphia: American Philosophical
Society, 1968), p. 59.

[8]See Eliade, Patterns in Comparative Religion,
pp. 265-80.

[9]Ghost Stories of an Antiquary (Penguin, 1974),
p. 67.

[10]The Best Supernatural Tales of Algernon
Blackwood (New York: Causeway, 1973), pp. 45-46.
Subsequent references are to this edition.

[11]I refer to the theoretical models of Levi-
Strauss and others, who atomize the supposedly
rational properties of myths. The ultimate effect
of this sort of artificial dissection is to empty
myths of their sacred content.

[12]See George Steiner, After Babel: Aspects of Language and Translation (Oxford Univ. Press, 1975) and

Ian Robinson, <u>The New Grammarians'</u> Funeral: <u>A</u> <u>Cri</u>-
<u>tique</u> of <u>Noam</u> <u>Chomsky's</u> <u>Linguistics</u> (Cambridge Univ.
Press, 1976).

[13]<u>The</u> <u>Flight</u> <u>of</u> <u>the</u> <u>Wild</u> <u>Gander</u> (Chicago: Regnery,
1972), p. 6.

3

FILM AS MYTH AND NATIONAL FOLKLORE

Paul Monaco

PURPOSES OF THE ESSAY

This essay addresses several ways of thinking
about films at the level of their broadest social
meaning. It takes as its point of departure the
notion of "film as myth," which has a long and often
obscure history. As with most "film as" formulations, the phrase lacks precision and has too many
meanings. A discussion and clarification of the
"film as myth" formulation will lead to consideration of a complementary, broader, and, it is hoped,
more useful notion--"Film as National Folklore."
The phrase "Film as National Folklore" has specific
origins but has been accorded little attention in
film studies, either past or current. The term
originated--in print at least--with Ricardo Canudo,
writer of movie scenarios, founder of the Parisian
"Club of the Friends of the Seventh Art," gadfly
commentator on the cinema, and author of a book
entitled The Image Factory (1927).[1]
Overall, the aim is to clarify a structural
approach to the history of film in light of the
framework of a history of ideas. The result will be
to sketch an approach to film that shifts attention
from the generally abused concept of "film as myth"
to the potentially more precise and productive

notion of "film as national folklore." This strategy moves away from the established aesthetic
approaches to cinema in which the emphasis is on
the film as a text to one in which more attention
is paid to the context in which the film is made.
The result is to diminish, for purposes of analysis,
the importance or significance of reliance upon the
individual creative work.

FILM AS MYTH: REFLECTIONS ON USES
AND ABUSES OF THE TERM

In the western world, since the early nineteenth
century, the popular uses of the word myth have,
with increasing confusion, come to stand for at
least two different concepts. One is the simplified
view that myth is anything that is opposed to
"reality."[2] The other, based on anthropological
fieldwork, connects myth in archaic or primitive
societies with absolute truth, or as Bronislaw
Malinowski puts it, "as not being merely a story
told, but rather a reality lived."[3] It is at either
end of this polarity that talk and thought about
"film as myth" has become mired. Rarely does the
focus shift between the two, and rarer still are
connections to the Jungian view of myth (with its
insight into archetypal and transcendent modes of
representation of collective desires), which might
be the most productive path for cinema studies to
follow.
The idea of myth as "anything opposed to reality"
resonates in studies that concentrate on the so-
called "escapist" elements of many feature films.
This abuse almost invariably strikes to a pejorative
conclusion. At the other end of the polarity film
studies tend to regard the striking pictorial accuracy of motion pictures as yielding prima facie
evidence that they must somehow produce a "reality
lived" for great numbers of viewers. Speculation
about the near-hypnotic effects of film projections
on viewers, or about the sense of absorption of the
movie-goer into the filmic action, however, are not
convincing proofs that the critical faculties of
viewers are so affected as to render film a "reality
lived." Yet this is the misassumption that many
applications of the notion of "film as myth" imply.[4]

A more fruitful insight into the kinship between
film and myth is suggested in an oblique argument,
that the type of fiction found in myth and film is
"specifically unharnessed, a basic prototypic
pattern capable of many variations and disguises."[5]
Myth, then, is by nature possessed of a special sort
of ambiguity. So, too, is the film. Myth represents the reflection of a certain kind of thinking
that creates a particular mode of being. This may be
true of the cinema as well. It is not so much that
the cinema creates a "reality lived," but rather
that it transcends reality (quasi-magically) while
maintaining a close connection to the pictorial
accuracy often associated with reality.

Myth, it has been maintained, makes use of a
special kind of imagination called--quite loosely--
fantasy. Fantasy is not limited to myth, of course.
But fantasy in myth may be characterized as tending
to exceed the mere dislocation of familiar and
naturalistic connections and associations.[6] What
is at issue is the concept of causality that is
special to myth. Films "think" fundamentally in
visual images; the introduction of language through
voice in films at the end of the 1920s has not
altered this truth. Film creates patterns of causa-
tion by manipulating temporal relationships visu-
ally. A connection here between film and myth may
be illuminated by reference to a provocative idea
borrowed from Mircea Eliade. In discussing the
myths of the modern world he points out that the
main mythical structures of the twentieth century
have to do with time. His view holds that the
mythical in the modern world attempts to get "beyond
time," attempts, in other words, to break through
time and produce a liberation from history. In this
context, Eliade makes a passing reference to "visual
entertainment" and reading.[7] He is referring to
"concentrated time" as experienced in both the
cinema and the theater.

The concentration of time in theater, however, is
in no way especially modern. What is, by contrast,
peculiar to film is the cinema's capacity not only
to concentrate, but also to "elongate" time. The
mode of discontinuous presentation within a film,
introduced through parallel editing, has been long-
since perfected to the point where almost no transi-
tions in time (unless badly or ineptly handled) are

too abrupt or jarring to be followed and accepted by
the movie-viewer.

"Film time" can be equivalent to what is called
"lived time," although this is rare; Cleo From 5 to
7 is one example in which two hours on the screen
are the equivalent of two hours of lived time. Or
"film time" can span decades, even centuries. Most
"film time" is "concentrated time," resembling a
mode of presentation common to the dramatic situation on stage. By contrast, the elongation of "film
time" is, perhaps, best exemplified in Sergei
Eisenstein's conceptualization and application of
montage. The "Odessa Steps" scene in Battleship
Potemkin is a notable achievement of elongated film
time. The sequence has been filmed so as to prolong
it over against "real time." The camera does not
follow the action but rather spots and reconstructs
the action so as to draw out from it the essence of
the scene by disregarding its actual temporal
rhythm. The "trapeze scene" in which the main
character, Boss, is tempted to let his rival
Artinelli fall to his death in E. A. Dupont's
Variety (1925) is a similar, though less classic,
example of this. It is its ability to emphatically
and easily manipulate time that distinguishes film
to a great degree from theater. It is the film's
capacity to overcome or disregard time that relates
it most closely to myth. Moreover, it is a rein-
forcing irony that discontinuous presentation in
films is juxtaposed to the fact that the presentation of films is continuous and meant to be uninter-
rupted. This is why film as a cultural form tends
to be nostalgic and sentimental. Regardless of a
movie's content, the mode of a film's creation (dis-
continuity) as opposed to the form of its presentation (continuity) relieves, rather than reinforces,
the tension that is historical. Hence, the motion
picture is antihistorical or, at least, ahistorical,
and thus exemplifies Eliade's description of the
modern myth.

In attempting to describe what might be called
"myth thought" it can be argued that myth is identi-
fiable as a form of "collective thinking." Individual thinking, which we have come in the western
world, perhaps quite mistakenly, to regard as the
source of the creative impulse in the arts, is
personal and ideographic. Collective thinking, by

contrast, is impersonal, archetypic, and prototypic. Individual thinking has as its goal the manifestation of individual perceptions and feelings. The collaborative creative work that goes into making a film facilitates its eventual existence as a reflection of "collective thought." The "auteur theory" as applied to cinema is thus not only historically inaccurate but also fundamentally misleading. Movies are not "authored" but are rather reflections of shared thoughts and structures. What the "auteur theory" could potentially reveal is severely limited. Patterns of identification might be established which would be useful in cases of attribution. This, however, is a gratuitous contribution since attribution is rarely a problem in film studies. It is possible to divorce the making of a film from the exigencies that require technicians, actors, crews, editors, and so forth. It is impossible, however, to divorce film from itself; its mode of manifestation will always be collective.

Films reflect a kind of collective thinking similar to that found in myths. By extension it can be argued that films originate like myths. Enrico Fulchignoni maintains: "It can be said that the primitive spirit did not create myths, but projected them. Thus, myths could be originally revelations of a preconscious soul, involuntary testimonies of unconscious psychic processes projected externally, and, thus, nothing less than allegories of the psychic process itself."[8] The notion of myths as collective fantasies relates to one way of interpreting motion pictures--in terms of their reflecting the tensions or latent concerns shared by the mass audience for films.[9] Elsewhere I have pursued this line toward an interpretation of the "group process" in a given society as reflected through popular films.[10] Here I want to strike a different note.

MYTH THOUGHT, FILM THOUGHT,
AND THE HISTORY OF IDEAS

In the study of the history of ideas it has been suggested increasingly that thought in certain fields may be more "collective" than we have previously believed. In the natural sciences, for

example, the predominance of "mind sets" and shared
models has been demonstrated as influencing the
"normal" scientific work of a particular period.[11]
Scientific thought is nomothetic (that is, relating
to the abstract, general, or universal statement of
law) and as such may be especially subject to collective thought processes. Myths as archetypal,
though unrelated in their creation to the methods
of scientific thinking, are rooted in a similar
mode of thought. They manifest the collective unconscious and are part of a group process.

Film is collective as well. The cinema develops
imagery and forms which will be responded to
immediately by the collectivity. In this regard
commercial considerations in film-making have served
to form a crossover from "individual creativity" to
collaborative creativity in film art. The thought
processes in the creative arts are normally
believed, in our culture, to lead to the creation
of that which is unique, nonrecurrent, and responded
to at the level of appreciation and identification
primarily on the basis of analogy to the self.[12]
Individual "genius" responded to by individual
"sensibility" is the abiding catchphrase describing
aesthetic experience as envisioned in the western
world since the Renaissance.

"Myth thinking" and "film thinking" are related
to the creativity that occurs in associative col-
lectivities (such as the "scientific community").
But in film-making, collaboration on the producing
end is transformed through the societal response to
the filmic text itself into a mode of "collective
thinking." The associative groupings of film-
makers tend to be small and self-contained (for
example, "Hollywood Babylon," the German "Filmwelt"
of the 1920s and early 1930s, or the Cahiers crowd
that has dominated contemporary French cinema). The
creative atmosphere and ambiance for film-making is,
thus, more "primitive" than in the other arts.
"Primitive" here implies no pejorative commonplace
misuse of the term but simply refers to the structure of a type of community.

Definitionally, film-making tends to be archetypic, collective, and national. Each of these
terms has a unique meaning; taken together they
posit a total description of the "group process"
involved in film-making and the audience response

to films. Film functions as one element in the
broader fantasy life (or "myth life") of any collectivity to which it appeals. That collectivity
is, for better or worse, in the twentieth century
nationally determined. "For it makes little difference where one finds oneself in the contemporary
world--in Stockholm or Peking, London or New York.
Regardless of location, it is certain that every
'citizen' has, in the government of his or her
'nation,' a fantasy partner who cannot be excluded
from life's largest or most trivial endeavors."[13]
The history of the cinema must be written against
this backdrop. And that backdrop is the touchstone
for our comprehension of a felicitous appreciation
of the meaning of the title of this essay: "Film as
Myth and National Folklore."

Persons desire knowledge and wish-fulfillment in
regard to visions of society. Insofar as the
societies of the film age are accurately described
as national ones the mythocontent and mythostruc-
ture of films function as elements of national
folklore. Moreover, since the motion picture
possesses elements of fantasy of a certain sort
based on the suspension of time, and aspects of
wish-fulfillment which are collective, these function primarily at the level of national society.

FILM AS NATIONAL FOLKLORE

Ricardo Canudo claimed that film was "national
folklore." While he elaborated only marginally on
the notion, this conceptualization points in three
directions: (1) film as secular (a displacement
from the religious or sacred qualities often present
in myth proper); (2) film as being of the folk (that
is, appealing to the broad populace and expressing
widely shared ideas and attitudes through the
pressure of audience taste); (3) film as "lore"
(establishing the cinema as a corpus of works from
which derives a collective meaningfulness beyond the
significance of any single film). Insofar as the
term folklore was created in the early nineteenth
century to distinguish popular tales (of the folk)
from myths (which originate with aristocratic or
priestly elites) the word descriptively fits the
cinema well, but not perfectly.[14] Elites create

films, but they do so in a symbiotic relationship with the broad public for movies. The cinema is, then, a folk art at one remove. Folklore is an elaboration of the concept of myth, a broader term that subsumes myth within it. Likewise, the cinema, though containing myth-like elements, represents a broadening out from myth to folklore.

The only possible way to describe what such a theoretical understanding may lead to in terms of the actual study of film history is through examples. History here is meant not as the mere chronicling of cinematic events systematically, but rather as the comparative analysis of experiences of the past. In so brief an essay, examples can only be sketched in the roughest of outlines.

Let us look, then, at several instances of important innovative cinema: German Expressionism in the early 1920s; Soviet Expressive Realism in the late twenties; the "école réaliste française" of the late 1930s; Italian Neo-Realism following World War II; and the French "New Wave" of the late fifties and early sixties. This choice is selective but not arbitrary. The list could include, of course, other "great" cinema periods. But it is only necessary that the reader agrees that each of these cinemas represents a flourish of creative and imaginative innovation in film-making.

If we try to grasp the context of each of these epochs in terms of a superficial and intentionally provocative thumbnail sketch, several elements draw our attention immediately. In trying to account for bursts of creative film activity, one suggestion that has been previously advanced, in a number of places, is that the economic conditions under which these cinemas operated determined their originality and innovation in film production. For example, the argument has been made that French film-makers of the late 1930s benefited from a weak film industry from which large producers were excluded or had excluded themselves.[15] This seems suspect for several reasons, however. The French film industry throughout the 1920s was as weak, and big producers shied away, to be sure, yet an innovative and imaginative national cinema did not result. (Only from 1930 to 1934 was the French cinema commercially stronger, but while production increased during these four years, the overall strength of the industry during this short period should not be exaggerated.) To shift the focus within a comparative framework poses even greater problems for this sort of economic explanation. The film industry conditions under which the "New Wave" emerged in France were not similar to those of the late 1930s. At the end of the 1950s, state aid in France permitted the production of documentaries and thus created many training opportunities for young film-makers. In 1959 twenty-four directors made their first feature films, and in 1960 the number was forty-three. The earliest "New Wave" films were enormous box-office successes.[16]

The German cinema immediately after World War I was also in good shape financially; even the runaway monetary inflation of the years 1922 and 1923 did little to harm film producers. The majority of the classic expressionist films were produced by UFA (Universum Film, A.B.) and other large companies that had access to stable sources of financial support. Indeed, much of the backing for UFA and the other major film-producing firms came from traditional and well-established sources of German investment capital: Ruhr industrialists, major banks, shipping and insurance companies, brokerage houses, and investment firms.[17]

The Italian Neo-Realist directors operated under unstable economic conditions, and, to some degree, so did the Soviet film-makers of the mid- and late twenties. But conditions in the Soviet film industry between 1924 and 1930 were not as dire as those which existed in post-World War II Italy. In the Soviet Union during the 1920s, the financial investment in movies increased apace and the condition of production facilities improved steadily, if not dramatically; to believe otherwise is to swallow the Stalinist line that in no area of the Soviet economy did productivity increase until the Draconian measures of the First Five Year Plan took effect.[18]

To summarize, a common economic model does not hold in explaining the bursts of creativity in these five different cinema epochs. Two of these cinemas were relatively poor and characterized by small, independent producers. Two others were well off financially and stabilized, and the fifth stood somewhere in between. Theoretically, a wealthy film industry may be able to release some "excess

profits" for "high risk" or "prestige" productions.
An economically poor cinema may lack firmly en-
trenched industrial structures, thus encouraging
more independent "high risk" productions. No single
explanation of the relationship between economic
conditions in a film industry and its creativity
holds. It would take a major effort in structural
analysis and the modeling of a shifting paradigm to
clarify the dynamics of that relationship.

A striking element that is common to these five
epochs of innovative cinema is that each occurred
during a period of national humiliation or tortured
self-contradiction in the film-producing society.
Germany after 1918 was humiliated by defeat, accused
as a nation of war guilt, and treated as a pariah in
the international community. Expressionism in the
German film flourished in the years when these
dilemmas were most intense. After 1924 the Dawes
Plan led to financial recovery, stabilization of the
currency, and increasing international reacceptance
and reconciliation for Germany. And after 1924
Expressionism in the German cinema waned.

The Soviet Union was confronted in the mid-1920s
by a fast-emerging paradox that threatened the very
basis of society. After 1924 the ideological notion
of internationalism was challenged by the pragmatic,
and fundamentally nationalistic, credo of "Socialism
in One Country." It was immediately after Stalin's
promulgation of this slogan as policy in 1924, and
during the next five or six years, that Expressive
Realism flourished in the Soviet cinema. The view
that its end came because of repressive measures
directed at the film industry can be challenged by
the alternative interpretation that Expressive
Realism ended because by 1930 the Soviet Union was
on the way to asserting its own national will
through the self-image of an increasingly successful
society in which socialist industrialization had
established itself as the way of the future.

In France the year 1934 marked the belated impact
of the international capitalist economic Depression,
but it also saw the near-outbreak of civil war.
France, having been to the brink of civil war,
remained a torn, divided, and polarized nation
during the years 1934 to 1940, when her film-makers
made a number of outstanding contributions to
imaginative and innovative cinema.

Clearly, Italian Neo-Realism, like German Expressionism, developed in a period that followed defeat
in war. In Italy, however, the national idea had
been discredited during the Second World War, whereas the German national idea--it is safe to say--was
only marginally discredited, and at that only in
certain segments of the German society, during World
War I. The Italian situation was, moreover, complicated by the fact that Italy had rebuked her Fascist
leadership, broken the partnership with Nazi
Germany, and reached separate terms of peace with
the Allied Powers. Still, Italy was treated as an
enemy belligerent in the peace settlements after the
war (1946-47). The conflict between national humiliation and a coming to terms with it was furthermore
complicated by the virtual eclipse of Europe after
1945 from her place of previous preeminence in
world affairs.

The French "New Wave" can be dated from 1959, for
it is usually agreed that the Cannes Festival of
that year marked its emergence. Hence, it appeared
just as the Fourth Republic collapsed under the
pressures of the war in Algeria, another instance of
national self-torment, polarization, and incipient
humiliation. The "New Wave" flourished into the
mid-sixties, or until shortly after the Algerian
question had been resolved. France had liberated
herself from the collective emotional turmoil produced by the Algerian situation and, in the process,
the Gaullist regime had established itself on a firm
footing, reasserting national integrity with a
vengeance.

CONCLUSIONS

Do these five examples yield a model of the context in which especially creative and innovative
cinema may develop? The presence of crises of
national self-image does not, of course, guarantee
the advent of creativity in the film industry. But
it does seem that innovative and creative cinema
may be precipitated by such national crises. Would
not the cinema of the United States in the early
1930s and the late 1960s exemplify the model? But
the major insight here concerns the value and
accuracy of perceiving film itself as a form of

national folklore whose mythic elements resonate
from actual or perceived crises within the national
societies in which films are produced.

It can be said with historical accuracy that the
mode of "normal" film-making has been national. And
it has been folkloric in that national genres pre-
dominate, national standards of commercial estima-
tion and artistic evaluation hold in the first
instance, and films originate through a symbiosis
of those who put up the money, those who make the
films, and those who see them. Like myths, films
represent a mode of collective thinking.

It is plausible that because of the kinship of
film and myth, film functions so as to relate
closely to the paradoxes and tensions of national
crisis and self-contradiction. The even broader
notion of film as national folklore is heuristic.
It leads us to consideration of the myth-like
structure of films in a framework that has not
been explored previously. The evidence that has
been surveyed in this essay suggests that innovative
and creative cinema occurs when the mode of "normal"
national film-making breaks down as a result of
extensive crises within a national society. This
breakdown occurs because of contradiction in the
national consciousness to which film as national
folklore addresses itself under normal circumstances. What resulted, interestingly, in each of
the five examples cited was a cinema with excep-
tional international appeal whose sources of inspiration were rooted in the myth-like and folkloric
exploration of an internal societal tension. This
paradox may underscore the extent to which the
cinema is perceived unconsciously by the populace
as related to the tension of national identity.
This perception is unarticulated and muted, which
is no denial of its presence; indeed, the lack of
formalized recognition may well mark the deeper
meaning implicit in this aspect of film's function.

The cinema emerged and developed in the period
1895-1940. This was an era of strident and self-
conscious nationalism and aggressive chauvinism in
the industrial world. The history of film is, then,
related necessarily to questions of national consciousness. The subsequent development of the
cinema has carried the medium beyond categories of
conceptualization which might be considered nation-

al. Nonetheless the historic and structural matrix
in which film existed, and to a great degree continues to exist, is national. The notion of film
as myth and national folklore is a useful starting
point not only for analysis of the function of film
in the society for which it is created, but also for
analysis of the nature of the medium itself.

NOTES

[1] Ricardo Canudo, L'Usine aux images (Geneva,
1927).

[2] See, for example, the discussions in Thomas A.
Sebeok, ed., Myth: A Symposium (Bloomington, 1958);
a more complex treatment of myth as perceived
through the perspective of German Idealism is found
in Ernst Cassirer, Das mythische Denken (Berlin,
1925).

[3] Bronislaw Malinowski, Myth in Primitive Psychology (Westport, Conn., 1926), p. 11 and passim.

[4] Treated from an artistic point of view this
matter is fully discussed in Carl Vincent,
L'Histoire de l'art cinématographique (Brussels,
n.d., 2d ed.), especially pp. x ff., and in Elie
Faure, "The Art of Cineplastics," in Daniel Talbot,
Film: An Anthology (Berkeley and Los Angeles, 1967),
pp. 12 ff. A sound discussion of the realistic
impact of motion pictures on views from the perspec-
tives of psychology and physiology is found in
Y. Galfriet and J. Segal, "Cinéma et physiologie
des sensations," Revue Internationale de Filmologie
2 (1945), 289-93.

[5] Parker Tyler, Magic and Myth of the Movies
(New York, 1947), pp. ix, x.

[6] G. S. Kirk, Myth: Its Meaning and Function in
Ancient and Other Cultures (Berkeley, Los Angeles,
and London, 1970), p. 268.

[7] Mircea Eliade, Myths, Dreams, and Mysteries,
trans. by P. Maigret (New York, Evanston, San
Francisco, and London, 1960), pp. 34-38.

[8]Enrico Fulchignoni, La Civilisation de l'image
(Paris, 1969), p. 229.

[9]This mode of interpretation develops normally
along neo-Freudian lines. Especially informative
in terms of theory is Otto Rank, Der Kunstler,
(Berlin, 1909) and C. J. Jung and C. Kerenyi, Essays
on a Science of Mythology (New York and Evanston,
1962). A cautious consideration of the potentiality
of interpreting films as collective fantasies is
found in Raymond deBecker, "Pour un psychanalyse
du cinéma," La Table Ronde 109 (January, 1957), 79-
89. Theory into practice has previously been
attempted by two works, both written over a quarter
of a century ago: Siegfried Kracauer, From Caligari
to Hitler (Princeton, 1947) and Martha Wolfenstein
and Nathan Leites, Movies: A Psychological Study
(Glencoe, 1950). Most controversial and problematic
in interpreting myths or films as reflecting collective fantasies is the notion of an unconscious
or preconscious mental state assumed by such
studies. This is a question to which researchers
in the field must address themselves next, directly.
Even the most thorough treatment of the subject,
Walter Abell, The Collective Dream in Art (New York,
1966) has little to say on this matter. Clearly,
it is my own conviction that Freud overestimated
the degree to which tension is suppressed and failed
to admit that the fact that problems are not always
recognized immediately for what they are does not
necessarily mean that their source is conflict that
exists at a level deeper than that of normal consciousness. Psychic material is likely closer to
the surface of conscious awareness than Freud and
his followers in the analytical school have maintained. At both the individual and the collective
levels certain material is related to differently
and come to terms with differently than other
material. This issue must be dealt with in psycho-
social research. To begin from the Freudian point
of departure, however, by maintaining the existence
of an unconscious at the beginning of a research
question is a habit that must be replaced by a new
and more creative approach.

[10] Paul Monaco, Cinema and Society: France and Germany During the Twenties (New York, Oxford, and Amsterdam, 1976).

[11] Thomas Kuhn, The Structure of Scientific Revolutions, 2d ed. (Chicago, 1970).

[12] Still compelling in this regard is the Bergsonian argument that "true" knowledge (as opposed to empirical, scientific knowledge) is attained only through an intuitive sense of analogy to the self: Henri Bergson, Introduction à la métaphysique (Paris, 1903). Also of interest in regard to some of the issues raised in this paper is the essay in which he deals with questions related to the mode of thinking and myth: Henri Bergson, Two Sources of Morality and Religion, trans. C. Brereton and R. A. Audra (New York, 1935).

[13] Henry Ebel has commented on this element of the group process in various articles in The Journal of Psychohistory from 1976 to the present.

[14] Charles William Brooks, "Jean Renoir's 'Rules of the Game,'" French Historical Studies 7 (1971) 265, 266.

[15] Penelope Houston, Contemporary Cinema (Middlesex, 1966), pp. 100-103.

[16] Walter Dadek, Die Filmwirtschaft (Freiburg im Br., 1957) and Alexander Jason, Jahrbuch der Filmindustrie (Berlin, 1923 [vol. I] and 1926 [vol. II]); see also, Monaco, op cit., pp. 26-31.

[17] George Huaco, The Sociology of Film Art (New York and London, 1965) attempted a comparative model of artistic creativity for Germany, 1920-31, the Soviet Union, 1925-30, and Italy, 1945-55. His approach begins from a different perspective than the one I take here and develops quite differently from mine throughout. For material on the Soviet cinema see Jay Leyda, Kino (New York, 1973), especially pp. 193-276.

[18] Earl W. Count, "Myth as World-View," in Edward Diamond, ed., Cultural History (New York, 1960), pp. 596 ff.

4

FELLINI: MYTHIC AND POSTMYTHIC

Frank Burke

There is probably no better witness to the richness and life of Fellini's movies than the vital
activity of myth within them. Universally acknowl-
edged but seldom discussed seriously by commentators
on Fellini's work, myth is central to Fellini's
vision. In fact, his most sophisticated films work
with myth in as many as three different ways. They
embody both a mythic and a postmythic dimension.
(The latter is the mythic dimension transformed;
it includes the mythic but liberates it from some
of its conservative tendencies.) The mythic dimension itself consists of two radically different
facets and activities of myth.

THE MYTHIC DIMENSION

The mythic dimension of Fellini's work is comprised of what might be termed "myth as inherited
value," and it has a conservative and a liberating,
a prescriptive and a heuristic function in his
films. As a conservative and prescriptive force
it is the embodiment or entombment of the past--of
ideals, norms, beliefs, traditions, and archetypal
modes of perception imposed on Fellini's characters
by their social, historical, religious, and psycho-

50

logical heritage. It usually manifests itself as
an institutional force in Catholicism and Fascism
and as a psychological or archetypal force in
"momism"--the individual's distortion of life
through the perception of Woman (and numerous other
Idealizations) as potential mother, capable of providing a womb safe from the conflicts and challenges of contemporary, individualized, existence.

Myth as the entombment of the past is a threat to
Fellini's characters, to his artform (movies), and
to his proclaimed and cinematically apparent vision
of life. As virtual mausoleums of outmoded ideas
and behavior patterns, the myths of the past
imprison Fellini's characters in abstractions and
fragmented lifestyles that render them incapable of
creative life in the modern world. As repositories
of fixed ideas, beliefs, norms, symbols, and stereo-
types--that is, abstractions that "staticize" life[1]
--they are the enemy of cinema, whose name and
nature affirm motion and whose imagistic immediacy
affirms the concrete, individualized activity of
the present rather than abstract, generalized ideas
from the past. Moreover, as storehouses of collective values (values not only of religion and politics but also of the collective unconscious), the
myths of the past are the enemy of all that Fellini
and his films seek to achieve: "I loathe collectivity. Man's greatness and nobility consist in
standing free of the mass. How he extricates himself from it is his own personal problem and private
struggle. This is what my films describe."[2] It is
myth as the enshrinement of the past to which
Fellini frequently refers when he insists that the
old myths are dying off and that he and his characters must vigorously assist in their destruction.[3]
And it is myth as the past entombed to which his
main characters fall prey in Fellini's more negative
movies (for example, Il Bidone, La Dolce Vita,
Amarcord, Fellini's Casanova).

If the only function of the strictly mythic
dimension of Fellini's work--myth as inherited
value--were to embody dead and deadening tradition,
all his movies would be orgies of annihilation (or
"decreation" to borrow a gentler and perhaps more
accurate term from Wallace Stevens). However, in
his more affirmative and complex movies, myth as
inherited value is present in a liberating, heuris-

tic, positive guise. It functions as the inherited
life of the "historical" imagination. Fashioned by
the creative imagination of peoples and cultures of
a prior age, the myths of the past bear with them
the creative energy that gave birth to them, and
they release that energy to those of Fellini's
characters who are willing and able to assimilate
it.[4]

Like myth as the entombment of the past, myth as
the life of the historical imagination is both an
institutional and a psychological or archetypal
phenomenon in Fellini's films. At times it is
difficult to recognize myth as a positive institutional phenomenon (as the life of the communal-
historical imagination) because the institutions
that embody it--Catholicism and Fascism--seem to be
merely negative and repressive. Nevertheless,
Fellini sees and reveals that, despite the decadence
of institutionalized religion and militarized political power, each was born out of a creative urge
which, though now perverted, was once quite positive. He perceives something numinous and vitalizing in the myths of and surrounding Christ that
gave birth to Catholicism, something dynamic and
energizing in the exploits of Julius Caesar, the
"Godfather" of Fascism. Consequently, the myths of
Catholicism and Fascism can and do impart to
Fellini's most successful characters a vitality and
dynamism which those characters transform into
personal, liberating, creative action.[5] (Fellini
emphasizes the creative, imaginative vitality of
traditional myth by revealing the immense amount of
art it generates. Painting, sculpture, poetry,
architecture, stage plays, movies, and even fashion
shows resurrect and celebrate the myths of the past
in Fellini's movies, using and renewing the energy
of those myths by embodying them in ever new forms.)

Just as myth in its institutionalized and
historical aspect can function dynamically, creatively, in Fellini's films, so can myth as a personal, archetypal power. For the mythic content in
the dreams, visions, and heightened perceptions of
Fellini's most creative characters are not merely
the neurotic and distorting products of an archaic
collective unconscious; they are evidence and
bearers of the energy that propels the mythmaking,
image-creating processes of the human imagination.

They are a sign not of the sickness of Fellini's
characters but of their astonishing health--of an
irrepressible instinct to create and, through
creating, to generate imaginative solutions to the
problems of their existence. Their health and
creativity are such that they are capable of assimilating the energies released by their archetypal
imaginations and of transforming both energy and
archetype into creative, personal visions that
liberate them from the hold of an archaic, collective way of perceiving and relating to life.

To help summarize and clarify the two functions
of myth as inherited value--that is, its entombment
of the past and its embodiment of the life of the
historical imagination--we might adapt Joseph
Campbell's view of the function of myth and ritual
in society: "Myth and ritual are embodiments of
civilization which protect the individual while he
matures. . . . His maturation is equivalent to
rebirth; he is released from his community's myths
without recoiling from them as frauds."[6] As a
storehouse of the past, myth functions as a womb
within Fellini's films--an enclosure that protects
but threatens to fixate his characters. And, as
the haven of creative energy, the "womb" of myth is
also (paradoxically) a vitalizing environment
inducing the individual to be reborn as an individ-
uated, liberated creature.

THE POSTMYTHIC DIMENSION

In describing the creative, energizing aspect of
myth as inherited value, I used the term "heuristic." Its dictionary meaning, "tending toward
discovery," accurately captures Fellini's sense of
myth or mythmaking as a creative, positive event.
For at the heart of the creative urge which fashioned the myths of the past, Fellini sees an impulse
to discover-through-creation the values and powers
that vitalize life. He sees an impulse to view life
as sacred, to see and affirm (as William Blake did)
that everything that lives is holy. In short,
Fellini sees mythmaking as the fulfillment of a
desire to relate with full creative love to life and
the life process.

Consistent with this, in Fellini's most affirmative movies his main characters are able to assimilate the creative, loving, "heuristic" urge alive
within the myths of the past and use it to create
value in the present. In order to do so, however,
they must use the energy of the old myths against
the myths themselves (or against the "structures"
of the myths). To live fully and lovingly in the
present, they must free themselves from the rigid-
ity, stasis, and irrelevance of prior mythic forms.
More than that, they must free themselves from myth
itself--or at least myth in its traditional guise.
For while traditional myth seeks to erect symbols
of lasting and communal value, Fellini's characters
live in a world of concrete and incessant change
and radical individuality--a world in which any
attempt to erect a value system that extends beyond
either the moment or the individual is reactionary
and absurd.[7]

Because of myth's inadequacy in the contemporary
world, the successful individuals in Fellini's work
must evolve a postmythic relationship to their
world by the end of their films. They must transform the creative energy they have assimilated from
myths of the past into the capacity to create value
in and for the moment--to satisfy their own (and
no one else's) moment-to-moment needs for individuation. The mythmaking energies of the past thus
become the postmythic capacity for creative, spontaneous, valuefull action in the present. They
evolve into the talent not for making new myths but
for "making do"--in the fullest and most dynamic
sense of the phrase.[8]

In growing beyond a mythic to a postmythic
relationship to the world, Fellini's most successful
characters free themselves not only from the institutionalized myths of the past but also from their
own archetypal distortions of and preconceptions
about reality. They liberate their world from all
mythic-symbolic content and allow their world to
radiate its own numinosity (not the numinosity that
was formerly projected onto it). They thus become
creative individuals living in a world of creative
individuality. Their imaginative energy is freed
from preconception to marry its world and the vitality of the life process itself. They perceive all
life as a sacred power whose energy and evolutionary

thrust is a form of love, manifest in and through
their own loving imaginations. Since they themselves have become loving, creative forces, they see
themselves as agents of the life process, bearing
its own powers within them, acting out its own evolutionary enterprises. All prior sense of dissoci-
ation, alienation, oppression, and containment
dissipates. All is open, all is possible, all is
free.

As a way of concretizing and clarifying some of
these generalizations about myth in Fellini's work,
let us turn to four of his most affirmative and
complex movies: 8 1/2, Juliet of the Spirits,
Fellini Satyricon, and Fellini's Roma. There occurs
within each a mythic or myth-related series of
events which constitutes a turning point in the
movie, when Fellini's main character employs the
creative energies he or she has assimilated from
the myths of the past to break free of those myths
and evolve a postmythic relationship to the world.
The existence of this turning point and breakthrough is, of course, what makes these films so
affirmative and helps to distinguish them from
those of Fellini's films in which myth is a primarily negative phenomenon, an inescapable prison for
his main characters. Interestingly, and in keeping
with our earlier suggestion via Joseph Campbell that
myth is a womb from which the creative individual
must be reborn, the breakthrough to the postmythic
in each of these films is accomplished through the
abandonment of a mother figure, a woman who functions (either negatively or positively) as a pro-
tectress for the main character.

8 1/2

In 8 1/2, the turning point occurs during the
press conference imagined by Guido, when he "kills
off" his former self by climbing under a table and
ritualistically shooting himself in the head. Immediately prior to the shooting, there is an image
of his mother standing on the beach, and the camera
eye (Guido's imagination) draws rapidly back and
away from her--constituting a rejection or abandonment of her. Guido's mother (much like his wife

Luisa, who appears in a bridal gown and is similarly
rejected just prior to the appearance of the
mother), has throughout the film functioned as an
authoritarian, demanding female, whose attempts to
"protect" Guido have been attempts to repress him.
She has been aligned with both the institutionalized, repressive myths of Catholicism (she's
associated midway through the film with the grim
and emasculated priestly authorities of Guido's boy-
hood) and with the archetypal, distorted, myth-laden
projections of Guido's repressed sexual imagination.
She is clearly a major source of the guilt he has
suffered as the result of his natural attraction to
undemanding, sexually exciting females such as
Saraghina and his mistress Carla. In rejecting his
mother and committing ritual suicide, Guido is
using a mythic pattern of death and rebirth and the
mythic-archetypal image of the "Terrible Mother" to
kill himself off as a son--both to his biological
mother and to Holy Mother the Church, which she
embodies for him. In so doing, he is able to effect
rebirth as an adult capable of living a mature,
liberated, individualized existence. He is also
killing off that tendency within him for projection
and symbolization which makes him perceive figures
like his mother as archetypes, laden with archaic,
fragmented values, instead of as individuals,
lovable and worthy of acceptance in and of themselves. (This is suggested when the words "what an
incurable romantic" are heard on the soundtrack
immediately preceding the shooting. Guido is killing himself off not just as a son, but as a symbol-
minded romantic.) In effect, Guido rejects his
mother as a symbol so that, in the closing moments
of the film, he can accept her as a unique, concrete
person from whom all of his own projections have
been withdrawn.

  Following his ritual annihilation of "sonship"
and romanticism--his casting off of the-world-as-
Mother--Guido marshals the creative energy that has
been manifest in his own mythmaking (archetypal)
visions and latent in the imagery and products of
Catholicism through the film. He casts off the
myths of the past--in particular the film he was
trying to make: a heavily symbolic, intellectual,
self-consciously "relevant" compendium of old myths.
And he liberates himself for a wholly new, concrete,

de-mythicized relationship to the people in his
world. He expresses this newfound relationship as
he addresses the images of his world: "What is this
change? What is this sudden joy? Forgive me sweet
creatures. I didn't understand, I didn't know. I
do accept you. I do love you. . . . Life is a holi-
day, let us live it together."

8 1/2 was the first movie in which Fellini effected a breakout from the mythic to the postmythic,
and the result of this initial breakout is some
obvious ambivalence on the part of his imagination.
For, following Guido's expression of his postmythic
vision of life, he visualizes and actualizes the
love he has discovered within himself through a
vision that tends toward the mythic. He envisions
a "mandalic" dance that seems to emerge more from
an archetypal imagination than from one that has
grown beyond archetype. There is, in effect, a
moment of regression, since neither Guido nor
Fellini can live securely and fully in the realm of
the postmythic. Nevertheless, a breakout has been
effected, and, tentative though it is, it is the
seed for the more complete breakthroughs that occur
in Juliet of the Spirits, Fellini Satyricon, and
Fellini's Roma. (Actually, the feeling conveyed by
Guido's vision, particularly when it winds down and
leaves us with an emptied arena at the film's end,
is that through this final "mythic" vision Guido has
cleansed his imagination--emptied it of archetypal
content and freed it for wholly de-mythicized vision
and creation in the future.)

Juliet of the Spirits

Like the turning point or breakthrough in 8 1/2,
the breakthrough in Juliet of the Spirits is accomplished through the rejection of a mother. This
occurs near the end of the movie when Juliet
retreats to her bedroom to escape the army of
(largely archetypal) images that has invaded her
living room. There she is confronted simultaneously
by two things: the sound of a voice beckoning to her
from behind a closed door, and the image of her
mother, forbidding her to respond to the voice. She
rebels against her mother, the door magically pops
open as the result of her act of rebellion, and

Juliet discovers and frees the bound image of herself as a little girl.

Like Guido's mother in 8 1/2, Juliet's mother has, throughout Juliet of the Spirits, been associated with the repressive mythology of Catholicism and the warped sexual imagination bred by Catholicism. She has been the consummate image of femininity prostituted to and perverted by a patriarchal world--the agent of repression for all that is potentially feminine, vital, and creative in Juliet. By rebelling against and in effect rejecting her mother, Juliet releases herself (that is, the image of herself as a little girl) from the childhood state of immaturity she has been fixated at as the result of her repressive upbringing. More important, she releases within herself the potential for unfettered development, total individuation.

As was the case with Guido, Juliet's breakout-- her liberation from the myths of the past--is brought about by the release of the creative energy she has generated within her own mythic imagination and assimilated from the mythic content of Catholicism. For the event in which Juliet opts for the CHILD WITHIN rather than the MOTHER WITHOUT is a mythic-imaginative event. Both child and mother are products of Juliet's imagination, generated to force a confrontation in which Juliet can act out her creative breakthrough. Like Guido, she uses the mythmaking powers she has acquired from her world in order to free herself from the straitjacket of myth itself. Having done so, she breaks out into a postmythic relationship to her world. Though she doesn't verbalize it as Guido did when he addressed the creatures of his world, it is evident from the aura of total love and harmony Juliet radiates as the film draws to a close.

Juliet's breakout is much more complete than Guido's. She doesn't retreat into a semi- or pseudomythic vision to conclude her growth process. And by the time the film ends, the mythic images that have obsessed her have vanished. (They have been, as Juliet's "Grandfather" suggests, merely her own inventions, which have outgrown their usefulness now that Juliet has evolved beyond mythic entrapment.) Juliet does not even feel the need to respond to the verbal spirits who assure her they are her "true friends." As the film concludes,

Juliet moves freely in a natural universe from which
all projections, all mythic symbols, all archetypal
preconceptions, and all myth-laden signs of Catholicism have been expelled. As Fellini himself has
said (in a statement that emphasizes the disappear-
ance of the mythic, the total assertion of the concrete, natural, and "real"): "It is as if she no
longer cared about the origins of the sounds, the
images she has seen, whether they be part of a
natural mystery or part of a supernatural secret.
Everything in her is now anchored in peaceful harmony, beyond the mystifying ghosts that have until
now besieged her: she is concerned with the daily
miracle of simple reality.
    Juliet smiles, liberated, at peace."9

Fellini Satyricon

    In Satyricon, the turning point comes about when
Encolpio is confronted with the blatant failure and
degeneration of myth in his world. First of all,
Hermaphrodite, whose presumed mythic powers were to
assure Encolpio of wealth, proves to be a helpless
creature, incapable of withstanding the heat of the
sun. Then the "myth of the Minotaur," enacted under
the eye of a degenerate proconsul, proves to be
merely a "joke" which either reverses or destroys
all the values and relationships of the original
Minotaur myth. The Minotaur is a man, not a bull;
"Theseus" is a "student," not a competent warrior;
the Minotaur, not Theseus, wins the battle; and the
reward for surviving the labyrinth is not something
of genuine mythic value; it's a roll in the hay with
a vulgar and venereal Ariadne.
    As part of his confrontation with the failure and
degeneration of myth, Encolpio experiences his own
failure as a mythic figure--that is, his inability
to perform creatively by reliving the myths of the
past. Not only does he lose Hermaphrodite to the
sun and fail in his battle with the Minotaur, he
even fails in his attempts to make love to Ariadne.
Devitalized and meaningless, the myths of the past
fail to inspire Encolpio to deeds of mythic propor-
tion. Worse than that, degenerate to the point of
total impotence, they actually rob Encolpio of his
potency.

Confronted with the failure of existing myth and with the more concrete and embarrassing problem of his own impotence, Encolpio is offered an alternative to existing or known myths: the challenge and possibility of imaginative creation--the chance to generate a mythic and imaginative solution to his problems that will ultimately free him from the devitalizing effects of myth. The alternative is given Encolpio at the "Garden of Delights" by an old hermaphroditic figure--a vast improvement over Hermaphrodite him(her)self--who tells Encolpio a tale about "Oenothea." Not only is Oenothea a "new" mythic figure--that is, she is not part of Encolpio's Greco-Roman heritage as were Hermaphrodite and the Minotaur--she is a creature of pure imagination. For as the hermaphroditic figure makes clear, Oenothea has no geographical location or home, no objective existence. She must be found by the individual (by Encolpio) somewhere "beyond the great swamp" (in the world of the creative unconscious).

Given the impetus to recover his potency through a myth of his own making, Encolpio searches out and discovers Oenothea. And when he does, it again is made clear that she is a creature of his imagination. Encolpio drinks a magic potion which renders him delirious or "supraconscious," and he envisions a creature who has three different manifestations--those of young lover, Earth Mother, and grotesque statuette. Clearly not a "real" or "objective" figure, Oenothea in her various manifestations is Encolpio's image of his own feminine powers in their loving, mothering, and potentially destructive aspects. She is the visible manifestation of the fullness of his creative unconscious.

Having created Oenothea, he "mates with" her in her image as Earth Mother and is reborn as a potent creature, fully in tune with himself and his powers for individuation. (Even the "mating" is presented as more an imaginative than a "realistic" act of copulation, for both Encolpio and Oenothea are clothed during it.) More important, having created a mythic-archetypal vision in order to restore the potency that had been lost among the death myths of the past, Encolpio evolves beyond a mythic world and a mythic relationship to his world. As the film draws to a close, the mythic-archetypal forms

which had abounded in his world (particularly in the
neighborhood of Oenothea's cave) disappear. Moreover, the human embodiments of the mythic--Ascilto,
the phallic power, and Eumolpo, the poet-bearer of
the myths of the past--die off. The final moments
of the film are strikingly naturalistic, as Encolpio
joins the crew of a ship and sails into the future,
at one with a de-mythicized world of sun, sea,
wind, and earth--a world freed from the mythic projections of the past and in total harmony with
Encolpio's postmythic powers and aspirations.

Fellini's Roma

   In Fellini's Roma, Fellini-as-filmmaker is
attempting to make sense of and relate creatively
to Rome. In order to do so, he engages in an
exhaustive attempt to examine the mythology of Rome.
(All history is mythology in a Fellini film.) He
also attempts to "explain" the city of Rome arche-
typally, by seeing "her" as a Mother and a Whore,
an Eternal Female incessantly giving birth and
protection to people and institutions. The turning
point in Fellini's breakthrough (as main character)
from a mythic to a postmythic relationship to his
world occurs when he senses his own entrapment
within the mythic and archetypal confines of Rome.
He finds himself imprisoned in a world of irrele-
vant myth and useless preconceptions--much as the
Princess Domitila is imprisoned in a decadent and
dying aristocratic-religious society that generates
the grotesqueries of the ecclesiastical fashion show
and that painfully begs the cold and distant image
of the Pope to "come back" as a meaningful force.
   Despite his growing frustration with his own
attempts to document and explain Rome via myth and
archetype, Fellini makes one last effort to do so
near the end of the film in an encounter with Anna
Magnani. He tries to "summarize" Rome by describing
Ms. Magnani as a symbol of it--"an aristocrat and
a tramp, a she-wolf and vestal virgin," and so on.
With a healthy distrust for Fellini's abstractions,
she remains wholly indifferent to his attempts at
symbolization and tells him to go home and go to
bed.

In effect, Ms. Magnani functions as Oenothea did for Encolpio--as a threshold figure between a mythic and a postmythic relationship to the world. For after her "rejection" of Fellini, he abandons all attempts to explain Rome and the myths of its past. He also stops trying to impose archetypal labels on Rome.[10] In fact, all voice-over narration ceases. Fellini-the-narrator (the myth-entrapped, archetypally-obsessed Fellini) disappears, and Fellini-the-camera-eye-imagination assumes full command in bringing the movie to completion. In doing so, he takes all the creative energy he has assimilated from Rome in all its mythic richness and invents (as Encolpio did) a force capable of propelling him beyond the world of myth, that is, beyond Rome, which has become synonymous with myth in the course of Roma. He creates and surrenders to the community of motorcyclists who balletically encircle the monuments of Rome--Rome's mythic-archetypal past--and then, breaking their mandalic circles, propel Fellini's eye and imagination outside Rome into the world of a postmythic, open-ended, imminently dawning future.

Like Guido, Juliet, and Encolpio in their movies, Fellini (as main character) in Roma has taken the energy assimilated from the myths of the past and used it to break through the boundaries of mythic perception into a new and freer relationship to life. And like 8 1/2, Juliet of the Spirits, and Fellini Satyricon, Roma has used myth as inherited value "against itself," as a liberating force that destroys its own fixed forms and equips the individual to transform the creative energy of the past into creative action in the present--action which, in turn, facilitates and ensures creative action in the future.

NOTES

[1]In his essay "The Myth and the Powerhouse" (John B. Vickery, ed., Myth and Literature: Contemporary Theory and Practice (Lincoln: Univ. of Nebraska Press, 1969), Philip Rahv attributes a "staticizing" tendency to all myth: "the one essential function

of myth stressed by all writers is that in merging
past and present it releases us from the flux of
temporality, arresting change in the timeless, the
permanent, the ever-recurring conceived as 'sacred
repetition.' Hence the mythic is the polar opposite
of what we mean by the historical, which stands for
process, inexorable change, incessant permutation
and innovation. Myth is reassuring in its stabil-
ity, whereas history is that powerhouse of change
which destroys custom and tradition in producing
the future--the future that as present, with the
fading away of the optimism of progress, many have
learned to associate with the danger and menace of
the unknown" (p. 111).

[2]"Playboy Interview: Federico Fellini," Playboy
(Feb., 1966), 55.

[3]One of Fellini's more apocalyptic comments about
the necessity for old myths to die off was occa-
sioned by a visit to America and recorded in an
Esquire interview (August, 1970): "I remember going
to the Electric Circus, with its dance floor aswirl
with multicolored tropical fish, the floor carpeted
with semi-nude bodies, and those enormous holes in
the walls from which four five six pairs of feet,
male and female, black white yellow, protruded.
. . . To be able to lose oneself in that caldron,
where everything is burning, and where the old
myths, and yesterday's utopias, are all melting
away, there is something sacrificial in that moment.
It is a total and ever so gentle suicide, a moment
in which a new way of being a man, and in which
salvation, is perhaps still possible" (p. 23).

[4]Cf. Joseph Campbell's remark in The Masks of
God: Primitive Mythology (New York: Viking Press,
1970): "the myths of our several cultures work upon
us, whether consciously or unconsciously, as energy-
releasing, life-motivating and -directing agents
. . ." (p. 4).

[5]An interesting example of a Fellini character
assimilating the creative powers at the heart of
Catholicism and transforming them into personal
powers of individuation is provided by 8 1/2, in
which Guido takes vitalizing Christian notions such
as divine love, grace, and salvation and employs

them as "guides" for refining his relationship to
his world and to the people in it.

An interesting example of Fascism serving a
creative purpose is provided by Fellini's Roma, in
which Fellini-as-main-character assimilates the
Fascist urge to conquer and colonize foreign territory and transforms it into his own directorial
capacity to make sense of Rome on film.

[6]The words are actually John B. Vickery's, in an
introduction to Joseph Campbell's essay "Bios and
Mythos: Prolegomena to a Science of Mythology"
(Vickery, ed., Myth and Literature, p. 15). However, though the words are Vickery's, they are an
accurate description of what Campbell has, on many
occasions, asserted to be the societal function of
ritual and myth.

[7]Traditional myth, with its tendency toward
symbolism, stasis, and abstraction, is largely a
literary phenomenon and has tended to evolve and
survive through the spoken and written word. The
postmythic dimension that Fellini and his characters
have on occasion been able to enter is a "cinematic"
world of concreteness, motion, visual immediacy,
irrational change, and spontaneous, self-generated
action. So, in moving beyond the mythic to the
postmythic, Fellini is evolving with and through
his medium of movies into a postliterary relationship to his world.

[8]Given the postmythic dimension within many of
Fellini's films, one might ask the question: what
about the films themselves--aren't they mythic
rather than postmythic? Certainly they have been
called mythic by countless reviewers and critics.
However, they are actually postmythic in precisely
the same way that the final actions of Fellini's
most successful characters are. As Fellini himself
has said implicitly and explicitly in talking about
his work, he makes movies wholly as personal and
momentary acts of individuation. He intends them
as neither symbolic, lasting, nor societal acts,
but rather as concrete attempts to work through the
problems of his own existence. Though as valid acts
of individuation they may be relevant to other
people and assimilable by them as part of their own

growth and individuation, Fellini's movies are not
intended to satisfy anyone else's needs for individuation. Also, they are not in any way intended to
be "accurate representations" of a stable, permanent
social reality or set of values that exists outside
the world of the film. They are acts, not symbols,
and are valid in and of themselves, not as reflections of any reality or "meaning" beyond them.

[9]Federico Fellini's Juliet of the Spirits, ed.
Tullio Kezich, trans. Howard Greenfield (New York:
Orion Press, 1965), pp. 180-81.

[10]The rejection of Fellini by Anna Magnani is
linked structurally to the theft of the 16mm
"documentary" camera from Fellini's film crew
moments before his encounter with Ms. Magnani, for
Fellini's attempts to explain Rome through the
imposition of myth and archetype have been, simultaneously, attempts to "document" Rome's past and
present.

5

FOWLES' THE MAGUS: THE VORTEX

AS MYTH, METAPHOR, AND MASQUE

William J. Palmer

"It is only a metaphor," Maurice Conchis, the
title character in John Fowles' novel The Magus and
the stage manager of the mythical, metatheatrical
masques that comprise a good part of the action of
the novel, cautions the bumbling hero, Nicholas
Urfe.[1] "The masque is only a metaphor," Conchis
later echoes himself (pp. 419, 458). Of particular interest in the above quotations is the use of
the debilitating word "only." It castrates a
sentence, renders an idea impotent, inevitably
diminishes anything with which it is coupled. However, as The Magus progresses, the diminishing of
mysteries, myths, "pseudosupernaturalities," becomes
the major concern of both Conchis the Magus and his
willing but skeptical victim-protege, Nicholas.
Conchis uses myths as metaphors, "only" metaphors,
as a means of illustrating states of consciousness.
However, as Nicholas Urfe realizes and explicitly
states, these myths, these metaphors, and indeed
all myths, are "Fascinating. But [they] explain
nothing."[2] Urfe comes to understand how people like
himself are even able to cultivate the ability "to
hide behind metaphor" (pp. 255, 266).
I introduce this diminishing view of the power
of metaphor and myth in The Magus to underline my
own skepticism about the power and value of myth

criticism of literature. If Conchis can say that
his mythic masque is only a metaphor, then I can
state that the vortex motif in The Magus is only a
myth. Like Nicholas, I've come to find that the
vortex myth, which is the central concern of this
essay, is "Fascinating," but I'm skeptical about
just how much it explains. This skepticism does
not arise from any doubt about the presence of the
vortex myth in The Magus. The myth is certainly
there, in almost textbook detail, but it is there
in the company of a legion of other themes, images,
myths, and ideas of equal importance. The vortex
myth is but a part, a rather small part, in our
understanding of the structural complexity of
Fowles' novel, in our divining of the nature of
Fowles' creative act. "Fascinating. But it
explains nothing."

For Fowles, and for all who at one time or
another, with greater or lesser success have attempted to write fiction, certain myths are a means
of giving definition to, of seeing more clearly,
of revealing analogically, one's own discoveries
about oneself and one's relationships with others.
The creative writer writes to create a "self," but
he must have some means of imaging that creation.
Unfortunately, new metaphors, as "only" as they may
be, are in short supply. Invariably then, the
writer must opt for the older metaphors, plots,
images. Much myth criticism singles out the act of
choosing older metaphors and stories as the structural and thematic, the Casaubonian "Key To All
Mythologies." Why must we make so much of myth?
In contemporary literature--especially the British
variety of Iris Murdoch, Anthony Burgess, Joyce
Cary, and John Fowles--all the indicators suggest
that the best writers consciously avoid mythic
structuring, instead using myth, which steals in
inevitably, unconsciously, as an expressive tool,
as "only" metaphor, or as a vehicle for ironic
parody.[3]

In John Fowles' The Magus, one of the central
metaphors is the vortex myth. But the vortex myth
is "only" one image among many for the central concern and experience of the protagonist, Nicholas
Urfe, in the world of the novel, and for the intention, fallacies aside, of John Fowles in the writing
of the novel. This particular myth is certainly

present, overtly recurring, almost intrusively
repetitive. It illustrates the nature of abstract
psychological states; it serves as an analogue (a
simile or metaphor) for situations and actions. It
does not, however, dominate either the structure or
thematic meaning of the novel. Fowles' use of the
vortex myth is stylistic, "only" metaphoric. But
like every aspect of Fowles' style, his use of the
vortex motif is meaningfully eloquent.

For Nicholas Urfe, the Greek island of Phraxos
is "a site for myths" and "the pattern of his
destiny seemed pretty clear: down and down and
down" (pp. 60, 63). Later, soon after coming to
Bourani, Conchis's enchanted, cliff-hanging mansion,
Nicholas writes a poem containing a line that reads:
"I am the fool that falls" (pp. 91, 95).[4] Thus, at
the very beginning of the adventure, the mythic
qualities of the events to come are signaled, and
the explicit myth, that of the vortex experience,
is defined. As Nicholas leaves Bourani after his
first mysterious weekend, he has "the strangest
feeling . . . , of having entered a myth . . ."
(pp. 153, 157).

At this point, having been initiated into
Conchis's mysterious world, having "landed . . . in
the center of an extraordinary old man's fantasies"
(pp. 139, 143) as one lands in the center of a
whirlpool, Nicholas feels that his familiar world
has suddenly changed, become unstable. He feels as
if the squalid, self-deceptive reality of his life
to that particular point in time-space has been
superseded by his falling into this new mythic life.
This instability of reality--"the absolute dissoci-
ation of wild Greece" (pp. 73, 77) as Nicholas
describes it--signals his fall into the down-
spiraling swirl, the vortex of the godgame.

Conchis's godgame is the series of metatheatrical
events--dramatic vignettes, scenes, told stories,
movies, tableaux--in which the barrier between
actors and audience is intentionally broken down,
allowing the audience to become participants in the
play itself. The effect is similar to the rock
musicals Hair! and Godspell, where the audience
joins the actors onstage to dance and celebrate.
It is also akin to the intention in Pirandello's
play Six Characters In Search of An Author, where
the distances and distinctions between actors and

characters, audience and participants, illusions
and realities are dramatically questioned. The godgame in The Magus is a series of metatheatrical
events by which the Magus or magician or metatheatrical stage manager tortures and tempts, coaxes
and cons, intimidates and involves his victim-
protege in the existential realization of intersub-
jective selfhood. That is, the godgame by means of
dramatic involvement teaches the protagonist-
victim-Tarot fool the ability, through knowledge of
the personal self, to establish relationships with
others.

Nicholas characterizes his own participation in
Conchis's godgame in a number of different ways as
poetic first-person narrator, but one of the most
striking and important images he employs is that of
the stumbling naif fallen into a swirling, spell-
binding vortex.

Though Nicholas understands neither the genesis
nor the meaning of the vortex that he has been swept
into, he does realize the importance of being there,
of becoming one with the swirl, of riding the whirl,
of passing through the vortex into new consciousness—the new shamanic existence of becoming a magus
in his own rite. As the godgame heats up and the
metatheater of Bourani begins to unfold, Nicholas
describes his existential predicament in images of
"plunging" or "falling" into a maelstrom or void
and images of the world "breaking" or "careening"
away from him. "You have me out of my depth,"[5] he
tells Conchis as they talk of being "elect." "I
took the plunge" (pp. 101, 105), Nicholas says in
description of simple conversation with Conchis.
"I . . . let my mind plunge into darkness, into a
world where the experience of all my life was dis-
proved and ghosts existed . . ." (pp. 139, 143),
he says later after witnessing the apparition of a
seventeenth-century murderer. When Conchis employs
his twin beauties for the first doppelgänger effect,
Nicholas describes it in cataclysmic terms: "The
world split in half" (pp. 196, 198). Even the
landscape becomes vortextual: "The islands trembled
shimmeringly over the sea . . . like spinning tops"
(pp. 365, 401).

Perhaps the most obvious imagery of the vortex
myth appears in the hypnotism scene on Conchis's

terrace. Nicholas, totally in Conchis's power,
feels that he is

> looking . . . down into space, as one looks
> down a well. . . . suspended in a dark void.
> . . . the dark wind blowing in on me. . . .
> I was transforming, as a fountain in a wind
> is transformed in shape; an eddy in water.
> . . . I was not receiving from any one direc-
> tion, but from all directions. . . . the eddy
> whirled. (pp. 225-27; 238-39)

Thus, Conchis whirls Nicholas off to visit other
worlds separated in time and space from their
present reality. In the vortex myth, the victim-
designate or initiate feels his world give way
beneath him, become unstable, start to spin. That
cataclysmic or psychologically apocalyptic experience launches the initiate into new realms of
magical experience or consciousness, purifies him
in centrifugal meaning and experience, then spits
him back up, allows him to emerge from his shamanic
initiation and to carry his newfound identity back
into the world from which he originally fell. Perhaps William Butler Yeats in his vortex poem of
holy fire, "Sailing To Byzantium," paints the most
vivid picture of this journey:

> O sages standing in God's holy fire
> As in the gold mosaic of a wall,
> Come from the holy fire, perne in a gyre,
> And be the singing masters of my soul.

The image of the vortex in The Magus is even more
overt in the final stages of the godgame, during
what Conchis calls "the disintoxication." Nicholas,
confused, frustrated, is so caught up in the whirling ambiguities and spinning relationships of the
godgame that he suddenly begins to experience the
existential nausea, the vortex sickness:

> My head began to swim, faces and objects, the
> ceiling, to recede from present reality; down
> and down a deep black mine of shock, rage,
> incomprehension, and flailing depths of
> impossible revenge. . . . Then my mind plunged
> sickeningly, as if I had walked off the edge

of the world. . . . I was swept away. The
whole of life became a conspiracy. . . . I
let my mind wander into a bottomless madness.
(pp. 434-42; 490-93)

Thus, the imagery of the vortex, the language which
supports this particular mythic approach, certainly
is present. As the godgame unwinds, Nicholas
realizes that the vortex controls him. He acknowl-
edges his own confused helplessness: "I feel as if
I've been too well spun in a game of blindman's
buff," he says.[6]
    However, the vortex myth can serve as a metaphor,
"only" a metaphor, for the structure of The Magus
also. Fowles' novel is comprised of three distinct
parts:
    1) The Preliminaries: in which the action of
character definition occurs before Nicholas departs
for Greece and enters the godgame. In this section
Nicholas tells about himself, meets Alison, takes
her to bed for a few months and then flees the
relationship.
    2) The Godgame: this section divides into two
sub-sections of action:
        a) the Masques/Stories,
        b) the Disintoxication.
In these two sub-sections Nicholas meets Conchis,
the story of Conchis's life is told, and this story-
telling is interspersed with a number of staged
playlets and tableaux which progress in elaborate-
ness and in the physical involvement of the "audience of one," Nicholas. Then Nicholas is subjected
to a number of psychological tortures and tests,
mind-games designed to raise his consciousness to
the point where he will realize his humanness and
thus earn a ticket back to the real world and a new,
more existential, human life.
    3) The Existential Return: in this section
Nicholas is put out on his own to apply the lessons
he has learned about self in the godgame. He
returns to London, finds Alison (who has supposedly
committed suicide but shows up anyway, stepping out
of a taxi in Athens), and takes her to Regents Park
to attempt to end the novel.
    The vortex myth functions most powerfully in
the two movements of the second section of the
novel, the godgame. This section begins with an

imagistic transition which has been noticed in a
much different context by Peter Wolfe in his recent
book on Fowles' fiction.[7] The transition from
Nicholas's conventional life of unbuttoned sexual
exploitation in Part One is accomplished by means
of an overt literary vortex allusion. That literary
allusion presents an image of Nicholas leaving the
old world, losing his equilibrium, and tumbling
into a whole new, much less stable or predictable
situation. Fowles accomplishes this transition by
means of a whole series of allusions to Alice In
Wonderland. "I fell head over heels, totally in
love with the Greek landscape. . . . , I felt as
gladly and expectantly disoriented, as happily and
as alertly alone, as Alice In Wonderland," Nicholas
says.[8] Even the "Cheshire Cat" shows up later.[9]

After that entrance the vortex really begins to
spin Nicholas. By Conchis's intention and conscious
design, the godgame is a vortex, a windtunnel for
the study and testing of Nicholas Urfe and for the
making of psychological and moral determinations
about his future. The Masques/Stories focus upon
the contrast between classical myth and twentieth-
century history. Conchis's autobiographical stories
follow the course of twentieth-century history
through the contrasting vortices of the two World
Wars and the interludes of psychologically disturbed
peace in between. The imagery of the vortex is
especially evident in the scenes in the trenches of
Neuve Chapelle in World War I, in the machine gun
bullets raking the town square in World War II, and
in the mythic meeting between Conchis and the mad
blind seer of Seidevarre. All of Conchis's stories
are told from a Conradian veranda frame, and each
story is a step in the preparation of Nicholas Urfe
for descent into his own personal heart of darkness.

The second movement of the middle section of The
Magus continues to whirl Nicholas deeper into the
existential vortex created by Conchis. The purpose
of the "Disintoxication" is to prod Nicholas toward
both personal authenticity and the humanness of
intersubjectivity, or, in other words, to teach
Nicholas to know himself and to love. For Nicholas
the "Disintoxication" is like the spin cycle in an
existential washing machine. Conchis has soaked
Nicholas in all the discoveries of the godgame, in
all the mystifications, and thus Nicholas must

proceed to have all the impurities that have been
shaken loose in his psyche by Conchis's Masques/
Stories spun out in the whirling tortures of the
"Disintoxication": his talent for sexual exploitation in the vortex of the blue movie/Naked Maja
scene; his psychological inadequacies in the vortex
of the parodic Freudian-Jungian symposium; his
existential inauthenticity in the trial scene.
Finally the possibilities within him for love are
flogged to the surface of his consciousness as he
holds the nine-tailed whip over the bared back of
his phantom lover in his final test.

The godgame of the second section of The Magus
is a novelistically contrived vortex. The action
and characters are set a-spinning with none of
them knowing when it will stop, if it will stop,
if they will ever escape. Nicholas says of his
relationship with Lily or Rose or Julie or June or
whoever his shape-shifting lover is that "it all
became a sort of game inside a game inside a
game."[10] Later, attempting to analyze his relationship with Conchis, he complains: "Always with
Conchis one went down and it seemed one could go
no further; but at the end another way went even
lower" (pp. 465, 515). At another juncture,
Nicholas's multi-personed lover tells him, "I felt
. . . we were only just beginning the real play
when we stopped."[11] And, of course, moments after
she croons that lie, the play, the godgame, starts
up all over again. Soon after that, just before
the reels of the blue movie begin to roll, Nicholas,
hung on a wall, realizes: "I had still not reached
the bottom" (pp. 470, 521).

Finally, in a scene in which, still hung on the
wall, Nicholas must watch his phantom lover, posed
as Goya's Maja Desnuda, make love to a powerful,
Othello-like black man, he realizes that "their
identities receded, interwove, flowed into mystery,
into distorting shadows and currents, like objects
sinking away, away, down through shafted depths of
water" (pp. 479, 529). At the end of section two
of The Magus, Nicholas is like Ishmael at the end
of Moby Dick. He has been swirled around in the
vortex and spit up again, a survivor who must learn
how to live all over again.

In The Magus the vortex myth and imagery form an
appropriate metaphor--though "only" a metaphor--for

the existential predicament that every mid-
twentieth-century being must face in order to become
real and human. The modern world is generally
hostile to authenticity, to self-definition, to
freedom. Machines, social conventions, and institutions support the tyranny of conformity and exploitation. Part of the message of Fowles' novel
is that man must somehow be cut loose from or fall
away from the grip of this hostile world if he is
ever to learn anything about himself or make any
progress in his humanness. But this is "only" part
of the message. In terms of myth alone many other
avenues still need to be explored in The Magus, such
as the structural use of the Tarot journey, which
metaphorically parallels the classical mythic
journey, the functioning of the myth of Icarus and
Daedalus, and the use of mythic material as the
object of satire and comic parody. The point is
that literary criticism thus far has barely touched
the meaning of The Magus, hasn't even ruffled its
feathers. Limited myth studies like this one may
well be "fascinating." But they explain nothing.
A more eclectic approach combining the mythic,
philosophical, psychological, formalist, and historical approaches is needed.[12] And even the
eclectically endowed critic will still have to admit
that, despite all his work, The Magus (and, for that
matter, all fine literature) is still "only" a
metaphor.

NOTES

[1]Dealing with John Fowles' novel The Magus poses
an aggravating type of critical problem. There are
two equally viable texts of the novel: the original
text and now a revised-by-the-author version in
which numerous changes have been made thirteen
years after the first version. I would agree with
Fowles, who writes in a foreword to the revised
version, that this 1978 edition "is not, in any
major thematic or narrative sense, a fresh version
of The Magus." Though a number of scenes are
expanded or totally rewritten, the major thrust of
his revision is stylistic, having to do with the

arrangement of his words rather than with the
patterning of his ideas. My essay was written
before the appearance of the revised version. In
my own opinion, the original version is the fuller,
more critically available, text despite Fowles'
misgivings about its style. Be that as it may, at
the time of this writing the publishing companies
involved have not themselves decided which is to
be the true text. The possibility exists that both
texts will remain simultaneously and indiscriminately in print for a long time to come. With all
of this confusion in mind, all quotations from The
Magus, both in the original (Boston: Little, Brown
and Co., 1965) and in the revised (Boston: Little,
Brown and Co., 1978) versions will hereinafter be
double noted--the original followed by the revised
--by page number within the text of this essay.
This quotation is from p. 165 of the first version,
p. 166 of the revision. In those instances in which
a quotation has been omitted or changed in the
revised version, I will comment in a note.

[2]This quotation, which appears on p. 232 of the
original, is omitted from p. 244 of the revision.

[3]The use of myth for comic purposes is presently
a major concern of a doctoral dissertation on Iris
Murdoch in progress at Purdue University by Rose
Mohan.

[4]The "fool" in this quotation is the Tarot fool
whose mythic journey will be examined by Ellen
McDaniel in a forthcoming essay in the Journal of
Modern Literature entitled "The Tarot Journey in
John Fowles' The Magus."

[5]This quotation, which appears on p. 83 of the
original, is omitted from p. 87 of the revision.

[6]This quotation, which appears on p. 211 of the
original, is omitted from chapter 34, which is
completely rewritten in the revised version. However, in the revised version, the "blindman's buff"
image is reinstated on p. 281.

[7]John Fowles: Magus and Moralist (Lewisburg, Pa.:
Bucknell University Press, 1976), p. 89.

[8]In this quotation, which appears on p. 46 of
the original, the words "head over heels" are

omitted from pp. 49-50 of the revision, where the
words "totally and forever in love" are substituted.

[9]This quotation, which appears on p. 191 of the
original, is omitted from p. 194 of the revision.
However, on p. 281, Fowles adds another allusion:
"as nonsensically blind as one of Lewis Carroll's
queens before Alice."

[10]This quotation, which appears on p. 270 of the
original, is omitted from chapter 43, which is
extensively rewritten in the revised version.

[11]This quotation, which appears on p. 412 of the
original, is omitted in chapter 56, which is
completely rewritten in the revised version.

[12]My own book, The Fiction of John Fowles
(Columbia, Mo.: University of Missouri Press, 1974),
makes some inroads on the philosophical, formalist,
and historical approaches to Fowles' fiction, but
much more work is needed.

6

FRANJU'S GNOSTIC MYTHS

Terry Comito

Les Yeux Sans Visage remains, fortunately, a
scandal, despite well intentioned attempts to
accommodate its atrocities to the norms of a rational liberalism. An attack on the arrogance of
modern science is a project with which we all feel
comfortable. But perhaps we would do better not
to avert our eyes from those elements of the film
that resist such easy recuperation. The approach
to any genuine mystery, after all, lies precisely
through what is most scandalous to our ordinary
sensibilities. And it is the word mystery I would
like to insist upon--in its root sense, mysterium,
as well as in its reference to the sort of popular
tale Franju has chosen to exploit. The power of
his films, beginning with the documentary shorts,
has always been a subversive power, subversive not
only of what passes for the rationality of daily
life, but also--and perhaps not wholly in accord
with Franju's own conscious intention--of the
laudable pleas for social justice which are their
ostensible burden. "It is always necessary,"
Franju has said, "to go beyond, to pass behind."[1]
The important question is what, exactly, in this
world of slaughterhouses beneath lowering skies,
of hospitals and deserted monuments, is being documented?

I shall argue that the anxieties implicit in the bizarre and seemingly inconsequential fictions taken up in Les Yeux Sans Visage and also in Judex are ontological ones. It is, after all, no accident that the surrealists should have been so powerfully drawn to the mythology of popular culture; nor would Franju be the first of their number whose art has failed, quite fruitfully, to discipline a fundamentally metaphysical revolt to the exigencies of revolutionary practice.[2] We need to begin by admitting that the scar left by Les Yeux Sans Visage does not permit any easy separation of a "critical" response from the nervous laughter or uneasy bravado of those who have stumbled upon it, dubbed, on the lower half of a double bill. Beyond all our attempts to rationalize the "logic of the plot--the reasons for the gore,"[3] it remains a film whose center, emotionally as well as chronologically, is the moment in Genessier's laboratory when Marie's flaccid eyeless face is lifted off--"a large graft, all in one piece"--and tilted forward for our inspection.

Rather than searching for "reasons," we must try to define the exact nature of the ordeal to which we are being subjected. Franju himself has rejected the term "horror." Les Yeux Sans Visage, he says, is an "anguish film": "a quieter mood than horror, something more subjacent, more internal, more penetrating."[4] Even the most banal evocations of isolated chateaus, with their secret passages and mad doctors, may have an unsettling effect, if only upon our nerves. But when mysterium becomes a "mystery" its terror has been domesticated, and the totally Other becomes no more than a tantalizing blur on the margins of a familiar world--no more than a picturesque shadow to be illuminated in a happy conclusion. It is not surprising that Franju should complain he has never seen a truly black film, only grey ones.[5] Lacking the theophany of the old mysteries, the moment of transforming vision, what the traditional horror formula delivers is the thrill, but also the mindlessness, of pure temporality. In such films or novels the present is constantly annulled by a dialectic of anticipation and surprise. The only real content of any given moment is its shivery intimation of what is still to come. The absence of this dynamic is what has

most bewildered the critics of Les Yeux Sans Visage
and Judex. These films do not startle us; they are
almost completely without suspense--without that
suspension of the immediate which is, after all, a
kind of irresponsibility, a way of passing the time.

   It is in this connection that one may speak, with
some exactness, of the "chastity" of Franju's style.
The action sequences of Judex and Les Yeux Sans
Visage are curiously uninflected, oblivious to conventional climaxes. The chloroforming of
Genessier's victim, for example, occurs quite without emphasis or excitement in either the score or
in the editing of the sequence. Franju's characteristically long and impassive takes accord to the
girl's expiring struggle no more importance than to
the slight awkwardness with which Genessier and
Louise contrive to carry the limp body, still in
its smart leather coat and white gloves, to his
laboratory. Or, again, in Judex: When Diane Monti
lies in wait for the ambulance, Franju does not
cross cut in order to arouse our anxiety for her
victims. Instead, the camera circles around the
false nun lying in the midst of a featureless landscape, and watches the dagger emerge from beneath
the cross hanging at her waist. The threat is not
in what is about to happen but in the image itself,
in what it makes immediate. Franju is concerned
not so much with events as with what he has called
"lyrical explosions":[6] moments that seem to open
onto a world beyond all eventualities. He has even
claimed that he does not rely at all on the sequence
of shots, since each one, he says, ought to be full,
like a wine glass.[7] We may doubt that he is in
fact wholly without interest in montage, but his
claim does point to the essential quality of his
images. The world they reveal is oppressive in its
very presence--its presentness, without thought of
a future or memory of a past. The "subjacent"
quality of Franju's mood derives, I think, precisely
from the way in which, while seeming to deal with
violent activity, he arrests time, creates a real
present in which the unchanging circumstances of our
lives become visible. The thriller's conventional
images of imminent menace are transformed into
tokens of an immanent anguish, the more dreadful
because it does not permit us the distraction of
what is only fortuitous.

Certainly it is in such images, and not in the
events themselves, that the short sequences between
dissolves in Judex, or the more meditative rhythms
of Les Yeux Sans Visage, reach their culmination.
Diane Monti's escape from the mill is significant
mainly for what it leaves behind, the birdlike
wimple abandoned on the edge of glimmering depths;
and even Louise's pursuit of her victims is frightening less for what we imagine is in store for them
than for what we actually are made to observe--the
intrusion into the frame of ordinary life, already
undermined by Jarre's disquieting score, of a
hunter's intense regard, a smiling menace. As
Gabriel Vialle has observed,[8] Franju's preoccupation
with the gaze, with a look (whether sinister or
horror-stricken) of dawning recognition, is appropriate not only to Les Yeux Sans Visage, but to all
his work, whose intention is above all to make us
see: to substitute for the dispersed and shallow
vision of our ordinary awareness a deep focus that
penetrates into the object, isolates it, and gives
it a pure form.

> The more an object is hemmed in, the more it
> is false. It is false because it is dis-
> figured by all that surrounds it. If one
> succeeds in disengaging an object from its
> surroundings, it recovers its quality as an
> object, and becomes strange and often quite
> phenomenal. . . .[9]

This disengagement of the object from its network
of habitual associations--which is to say, from its
use, from what we remember or anticipate--corre-
sponds to what I have already said about the creation of a real present in which the thing itself may
be contemplated. And it is important to emphasize,
as Franju himself does again and again, that "one
does not create strangeness, one reveals it" in this
very process of disengagement.[10] We are at the
opposite pole from fantasy, from the creation of
alternative worlds. Objects in Franju are strange
--the French word insolite is useful here--precisely
in their resistance to the habits and assumptions
by which we try to make ourselves at home in the
world. Objects are strange insofar as they are

themselves and therefore other than us, Wholly
Other, and alien to our own nature.

This has of course become a familiar theme in
twentieth-century art and literature, but I hope I
shall be able to make some significant distinctions.
The world revealed in these moments of explosive
clarity is in most respects as far from the "archetypal and dangerous reality" of which Artaud speaks
as it is from the purely transparent world, purged
of its "suspect interiority," which is the goal, if
not precisely the content, of Robbe-Grillet's fictions.[11] Robbe-Grillet has spoken of man "facing"
the world, but Franju is engaged in a desperate
interrogation. His camera thickens and intensifies
the presence of things, accumulating textures (naked
flesh beneath a raincoat; black branches reflected
in the sleek blackness of Genessier's Citroen),
superimposing sounds (a passing metro, the distant
barking of dogs and cries of birds), allowing movements (the prestidigitator's gesture or the sur-
geon's, the smooth curve of the parking Citroen or
the railroad's safety gate) to complete themselves
before us with a balletic precision. He creates
everywhere, in other words, that density of sensa-
tion, and the visceral response it calls forth,
which was presumably to be banished by Robbe-Grillet
in favor of a system of purely optical resist-
ances.[12]

Franju's images create their own space, their
peculiar climate, which is why they explode from
the quotidian. But while Franju might agree with
Breton's dictum that "existence is elsewhere," these
moments in his films, rather than delivering us from
the merely actual, as the surrealist imagines he
can, make stunningly clear the extent of our bond-
age. Even the dangerous archetypes of which Artaud
writes, however alien they may be to man's habitual
"customs and character," speak at some level to the
needs of his deepest nature.[13] But Franju's world
--the world to which the mystery of his films admits
us--is a world of rooms within rooms, without a
breath of air, corridors whose end we cannot see,
tunnels of dark trees, a world of stone walls and
of grey skies that press down like stone. The
famous encounter of the umbrella and sewing machine
is a monument to faith in the freedom of the imagination, its powers of derealization. But the

frequently cited scene in Le Sang des Bêtes when a barge seems to pass through a field of wheat testifies only to the necessity of a barge remaining a barge, however untoward the circumstances; and the image is strange precisely in the rigor with which it impresses upon us the "characteristic movement" of this object that goes its own way without regard for our expectations.[14]   The soft machines of Dali,[15] like the metaphoric imagery of the Dali/Buñuel Un Chien Andalou, represent the triumph of desire over matter, which dissolves under its influence like the young man's hand swarming with ants.   But in Judex, Morales' hand, dissociated from his body, is held in the firm metallic grip of Favraux's desk.   Franju's machines--not only Genessier's laboratory but the two Citroens, Favraux's car, the metro, the railroad trains, the assortment (in both films) of scalpels, knives, pins, hypodermics, and other instruments of aggression--are always hard-edged and implacable in their alienation.

This is why I have wanted to call the vision of Franju's films a gnostic one.   It is a vision animated by what Hans Jonas, in his analysis of gnosticism, describes as "the experience of a basic rift between man and that in which he finds himself lodged, the world."[16]   Two shots in particular stay in the mind as expressions of such an experience. There is a moment in Les Yeux Sans Visage when Louise, her face marked by an anguished awareness of the monstrosity in which she is involved, gazes up from the barren graveyard where Genessier has been disposing of the corpse.   All she sees is a passing airplane, its wing lights blinking alternately as it curves away, droning, into the distance.   Like all the inanimate presences of Franju's films, presences stripped of a comforting sense of their habitual use, the passing plane seems to announce some message, but in a language no longer decipherable.   And near the end of Judex, a stylized chase becomes the pretext for a shot of harsh stone walls perpendicular to the gracious facades of the everyday world.   The building is oddly floodlit, and four men in black capes are slowly making their way upward.   We may be reminded of Cocteau's Orphée, but this wall, vertical rather than horizontal, is not so much a passage as a barrier; and the shot

manages to suggest--once again, it is not at all a
matter of suspense, of nervous excitement--that the
men's slow buglike ascent is eternal.

What is most fearful in gnostic mythology is the
narrowness of the margin left for the self's authentic existence. The body and its passions, the
reason, even the moral sense are conceded to the
kingdom of the world, so that in the end the pure
spirit or "pneuma" can define itself only by nega-
tion--finds itself suspended, as it were, over a
great abyss.[17] The peculiar dread of Franju's world
seems to me to have a similar structure. The
alienation of which we have been speaking is not
merely a question of objects having the upper hand
(a metaphor rendered almost comically literal by
Favraux's desk); it involves also the way in which
the body itself comes to seem a machine, an alien
object. Consider for example the extraordinary
solicitude for corpses, especially in Les Yeux Sans
Visage, a solicitude that attends scarcely at all
to gore--it is not merely our squeamishness that is
being aroused--but rather to their bulk, their awkwardness, the way clothing tends to slide off them,
the noise they make when dropped, their doll-like
sprawl when we see them collapsed far below us, no
longer part of the same world. What is revealed
in such moments is the strangeness of the body, its
uneasy existence just on the margin of the inanimate. The knife handle protruding from Diane
Monti's trussed-up henchman and the scalpel dangling
from Louise's neck are grotesque memorials to the
body's violability by objects: the body is a thing
in which such instruments stick.

Louise's case is of course particularly atrocious
since the scalpel enters just at the point, beneath
her pearl choker, of the suture which has been
revealed as the secret of her fixed inexpressive
smile and her slightly too creamy complexion.
Marie's bandage-swathed head may be a more violently
striking instance of this film's preoccupation with
life without a face, but Louise's mask is even more
disturbing because, fashioned of actual flesh, it is
closer to the human expression it imitates. And
Christiane herself is ambiguous, frightening as well
as pathetic, to the degree that her own mask, together with her oddly angular, weightless gestures
and Jarre's tinkling theme, suggest that she has

become wholly a mannequin, moving with a life we
seem to recognize but cannot altogether fathom. It
is characteristic of Franju that he should exploit
not the horror of her disfigurement but the more
insidious dread of the mask. It is the dread, I
would argue, of being alienated from one's self,
from one's own subjectivity: what the mannequin confronts us with is the moment when human expression
hardens into the grimace of matter.[18]

Mirrors are unsettling for a similar reason. As
the reference in Judex to Lewis Carroll might
suggest, they often represent for Franju passages
out of the quotidian world.[19] A mirrored cabinet
slides open to reveal Genessier's secret laboratory,
where a large mirror suspended at an indeterminate
angle over the apparatus of the operating room
throws into question the structure of space itself.
We share Christiane's disorientation as she descends
from her white attic hideaway through a house full
of darkened mirrors toward this final confrontation
in the cellar. Yet Franju once again disappoints
the expectations our experience with the genre might
have taught us. He focuses on the discarded mask
rather than on Christiane's reaction to her unveiled
deformity. What the mirror reveals is after all no
more than she had already imagined, already glimpsed
(she has said) in windows or in knives, in whatever
shines: it is a black thing she carries about with
her, a mere absence. (The scarred visage we finally
see through Marie's blurred vision seems in fact to
be a negative.) The mirror does no more, in other
words, than confirm Christiane's sense of existing
at an unbridgeable distance from the face whose
likeness now lies discarded beside her--the same
distance she felt earlier when she looked at her
portrait while listening, also from the past, to
the voice of her lover over the phone. What is
truly frightening is the way she now turns to gaze
at Genessier's bound victim, seeing her own face
once again, but this time in living flesh, which
returns her stare with terrified incomprehension.
It is a confrontation that seems to exemplify with
a peculiar dreamlike logic Gérard Genette's remark
that in mirrors "the self is confirmed, but only
under the aspect of the Other."[20] And after the
operation appears to be successful and mirrors are
once again permitted her, does Christiane, her new

face caressed by Genessier and Louise, see any
differently? "I see someone who looks like me,
someone back from the grave." The mirror into
which she wonderingly gazes, even as we hear her
father whisper that the graft will fail, gives
back to her an image of a self she can no longer
recognize as her own.

We have by now, I think, virtually answered our
initial question about the operation scene. Perhaps it would be useful, however, to ask some
further, utterly literal-minded questions. What,
in fact, is so dreadful about the medical ritual,
the glaring light and Genessier's upright hands
snapped into their rubber gloves? Or about the
apparatus of clamps and napkins with which the
victim's face is prepared? Why does the grease-
pencil that lays down the scalpel's path evoke a
particular shudder when it circles the victim's
eyes? She is not, after all, in pain; nor are we,
I think, at this moment generously concerned about
her future. The dreadfulness of the scene, with
its slow tracking of the lifted graft, is that it
carries us--beyond our perception of masks and of
mirror images--into that moment of recognition to
which the whole film has been moving and to which
Christiane also is propelled: the moment when we
recognize that the face itself, any face, is only
a mask. The identity we present to others and to
ourselves can be stripped away, no more than a limp
piece of skin. It is the dread--the gnostic dread,
I would like to say--of our essential nakedness in
the world that explodes upon us in this central
moment of the film. After the operation, Christiane
looks no different than she did before, and her
eyes, like those of Marie from the black holes in
her toweling, stare out at us from as great and
haunted a distance as they ever did. The refusal
of the graft detected by Genessier's impersonal
scrutiny does no more than make explicit the necessity that the mirror image has already implied.
Eyes are without a face, those eyes which can see
truly, because faces do not properly belong to eyes,
any more than in gnostic thought the psyche is privy
to the griefs or aspiration of the spirit. The
tears that fill Louise's eyes when Christiane turns
upon her are as strange to her skewered face as
Christiane's own tears are--or her revulsion or her

dread and incomprehension--to the smoothly imper-
turbable mask down which we see them running. And
Genessier? He has tried to live by making his eyes,
encased behind their thick lenses, belong to his
face, take on its mechanical immobility and purpose-
fulness. But even he at one point removes his
glasses in a gesture of purely human weariness and
despair; and in the end the glasses shatter into
his eyes, shivering them open to vision, and leaving
him too (the scenario is at pains to specify) without a face.[21]

Gnostic myths characteristically fall into three
stages, which express, in terms of an individual's
history, three possible states of the soul. First
is a kind of numbness or slumber in the world: the
soul sleeps in matter or is deafened by its meaningless din.[22] Then there is an awakening, whose
content is dread and homesickness because it is a
recognition that the world is governed by a necessity implacably alien to the soul's freedom.[23]
Finally, in and through this gnosis, there is a
kind of liberation that consists, as Hans Jonas
writes, of taking negativity and alienation as "a
principle of praxis": the Unknown God, who is simply
the "negation and cancellation" of the sensible
cosmos, beckons to the "acosmic Self or pneuma,"
which becomes manifest in "the negative experience
of otherness, of non-identification, and of pro-
tested indefinable freedom."[24] A similar dialectic
may be discovered not only in the narrative of Les
Yeux Sans Visage but also in its spatial structure,
which is film's most fundamental presentation of
ways of being in the world.

Several critics have noticed the absence of the
usual moral judgments. There seems, in fact, almost
to be a kind of complicity between Genessier,
Louise, Christiane, and their "victims" as they work
toward the revelations I have been attempting to
describe. Each in his own ways does (as the Doctor
remarks) what he must do, which is enough to distinguish them from the police or the complacent fiancé,
who complains that he is doing all he can. The
mundane world of seeming contingency is, quite
literally, a shallow one: we watch prudence making
its awkward and inadequate determinations before
what appear to be two-dimensional canvas flats. The
very stiffness of the exposition at the police

station or at the fiancé's apartment suggests
Franju's contempt for what can be accounted for by
such means. The world of necessity, on the other
hand, constantly opens out into depths at abrupt
angles to the banal surfaces of fact. Tree-lined
roads become spectral tunnels; stairs and corridors,
passages to some unimaginable "Salle de Reconnais-
sance." The room at the morgue bearing this name,
to be sure, yields only a false epiphany, although
one that points equivocally to later recognitions.
Genessier identifies his victim as his daughter.
But it is true that Franju's "lyrical explosions"
characteristically involve not a lateral engagement
but a movement of penetration--a movement frequently
led on, as Franju has said, by the "wave" of Jarre's
score.[25] Moments of arrival or departure (like
those of Judex at the ball or of Louise at the
Palais de Chaillot) reveal disquieting spaces
between foreground and background; and Franju's
camera moves with his characters along passageways
or tracks back before their advance, tilts to reveal
heights or depths, pans around objects or withdraws
to place them in unexpected contexts. The depth
suggested by such means is something quite different
from what deep focus offers artists concerned with
human liberty--a free zone in which encounters
between people can assume their natural shape and
continuity. It is significant that in Franju's
films we move along but not through corridors. Like
Louise in the opening sequence of Les Yeux Sans
Visage, we can see, however intense our regard, no
further than headlights penetrate into a gloom that
renders indistinct whatever directional signs we
may glimpse along the way. What is revealed by
those movements that disintegrate the frame of our
complacency is not a goal but the sense of distance
itself. In this world of necessity, in other words,
space is not an expanse in which events may unfold
themselves--wanderers in these depths are generally
solitary--nor is it merely a system containing
objects. It would be closer to the truth to say
that it is the space created by objects, a revelation of the distances latent within them: meditative
space, the very form of the knowledge to which the
characters' extremity has driven them.
    The conclusion of one's wandering in such a world
does not come, as in most horror films, with a

return to the ordinary, to the safe place; it does
not come with any return to place at all. The
fluid, indeterminate space of the park into which
Christiane wanders at the end of the film, surrounded by a cloud of fluttering doves, must be
understood as the negation of all sense of place,
just as her final gesture of revolt is the negation
of the world's oppressive order. Jarre's theme
reasserts itself for the last time, triumphantly
now, and Christiane seems to come to rest, if any-
where, in the music, in sound rather than in space,
as she drifts through the ambiguously dappled light
and disappears into shadow. The mise en scène
renders hauntingly concrete the rather banal remark
of the scenario that her gaze is "no longer of this
world."[26] What I am suggesting is that her "freedom" in this last scene is the correlative not of
any change in the world, but of just that consciousness of alienation which the whole film has
effected. Or perhaps I should say that her freedom
is the dialectical result of that consciousness.
She is not of this world. We are free just so far
as we come to realize the strangeness of all that
would impose servitude, the absolute distance that
separates us from the realm of necessity into which
we have been cast.

This psychic distance--or more properly, this
spiritual or pneumatic distance--accounts for one
of the most disturbing elements in Franju's vision,
the peculiar beauty physical atrocity assumes under
the gaze of eyes to which it has become totally
alien. The severe and formal grace of the white
horse, in Le Sang des Bêtes, who seems to curtsy as
he dies is translated into something more lyrical
in Les Yeux Sans Visage, but without losing its
precision or rigor. In the last scene's rush of
withdrawal and disengagement, Genessier's mutilated
corpse is no more than chiaroscuro in the unsub-
stantial loveliness--trees, sky, baying dogs, turbu-
lent white birds--presided over by his wraithlike
victim and executioner. Yet there is always dread
at the heart of such beauty, since to perceive it
we must take our stand in sheer negation--poise
ourselves, as I have already suggested, on the edge
of nothingness. Critics have variously identified
Christiane's doves as symbols of innocence, of
freedom, or of madness. What is frightening about

the scene is the way in which all three of these
abstractions converge to define her condition. She
has asked the gnostic question "How far are the
frontiers of the world of darkness?"[27] and has
found in negativity her only "principle of praxis."
The doves are most fundamentally just what their
fluttering movement suggests, an expression of
indeterminacy, of cancellation and dispersion, a
rending of all boundaries. And the special "magic"
Franju has so often attributed to Edith Scob, this
"unreal presence"[28] who becomes the very norm of
the film's sensibility, is her ability to evoke the
peculiarly lyrical emptiness into which the gnostic
heroine must finally be released.

NOTES

[1]Freddy Buache, "Entretien avec Georges Franju,"
Positif 25-26 (1957), 16.

[2]Aragon, for example, speaks of "working at a
task enigmatic to ourselves, in front of a volume
of Fantomas, fastened to the wall by forks"; quoted
in Maurice Nadeau, The History of Surrealism, trans.
Richard Howard (New York, 1965), p. 92. Cf.
Breton's remark that films are "the only absolutely
modern mystery"; J. H. Matthew, Surrealism and Film
(Ann Arbor, Mich., 1971), pp. 2, 21-22. For
surrealism and politics, see especially Robert S.
Short, "The Politics of Surrealism, 1920-36," in
The Left Wing Intellectuals Between the Wars,
1919-1939, ed. Walter Laqueur and George Mosse
(New York, 1966), pp. 3-25.

[3]Pauline Kael, I Lost It at the Movies (New York:
Bantam Edition, 1966), p. 7.

[4]Quoted in Raymond Durgnat, Franju (Berkeley,
Calif., 1968), p. 83.

[5]Buache, "Entretien," p. 19.

[6]See Gabriel Vialle, Georges Franju, Cinéma
D'Aujourd'hui, 52 (Paris, 1968), pp. 12-15.

[7]Buache, "Entretien," p. 18.

[8]Vialle, Georges Franju, p. 34.

[9]Buache, "Entretien," p. 13.

[10]Ibid., p. 14.

[11]Antonin Artaud, The Theater and its Double, trans. Mary Richards (New York, 1958), p. 48; Alain Robbe-Grillet, For a New Novel, trans. Richard Howard (New York, 1965), pp. 15-24, 49-75. Since the value I hope these distinctions will have is a heuristic one, I am ignoring later (and quite different) formulations by Robbe-Grillet and his admirers.

[12]Roland Barthes, Essais critiques (Paris, 1964), pp. 29-40. Raymond Durgnat is particularly good on this aspect of Franju's films; see Durgnat, Franju, pp. 20-22; also Durgnat, Films and Feelings (Cambridge, Mass., 1971), p. 38.

[13]Artaud, The Theater and its Double, p. 48.

[14]Cf. Buache, "Entretien," p. 15; Bernard Cohen, "Franjudex: Entretien avec Georges Franju et Marcel Champreux," Positif 56 (1963), 10; also Freddy Buache, "Les Premiers Films de Georges Franju," Positif 13 (1955), 33-34. For the characteristic "openness" of surrealist imagery, see Mary Ann Caws, The Poetry of Dada and Surrealism (Princeton, N.J., 1970), p. 6.

[15]See Ferdinand Aliquie, The Philosophy of Surrealism, trans. Bernard Waldrop (Ann Arbor, Mich., 1965), p. 76.

[16]Hans Jonas, The Gnostic Religion, 2nd edition (Boston, 1963), pp. 251-52. On surrealism and gnosticism, see Jules Monnerot, La Poésie moderne et le sacre (Paris, 1945), pp. 78-96; see also the remarks on Franju in Henri Agel, Miroirs de l'insolite dans le cinéma français (Paris, 1958), pp. 151-58. The question of Franju's use of Christian iconography cannot be considered here. One can say, though, that he seems to regard Christianity in gnostic terms as the religion of the god of this world, "the great Archon, whose dominion extends to the firmament, who believes that he is the only God" (Jonas, p. 134).

[17]Jonas, Gnostic Religion, pp. 123-24. Rudolph
Bultmann, Primitive Christianity in its Contemporary Setting, trans. R. H. Fuller (New York, 1956),
pp. 165-68, discusses negative transcendence in
gnostic thought; also G. Van der Leeuw, Religion in
Essence and Manifestation, trans. J. E. Turner
(New York, 1963), pp. 308-22.

[18]Cf., for the surrealists' preoccupation with
mannequins, Frederic Jameson, Marxism and Form
(Princeton, N.J., 1971), pp. 103-105.

[19]Cf. Vialle, Georges Franju, pp. 30-32.

[20]Gerard Genette, Figures I (Paris, 1966), p. 22.
Cf. Northrop Frye, The Secular Scripture (Cambridge,
Mass., 1976), p. 117, for mirrors and the "night
world" where the self becomes an object.

[21]In Vialle, Georges Franju, p. 128.

[22]Jonas, Gnostic Religion, pp. 68-74.

[23]Ibid., pp. 43, 130-46, 250.

[24]Ibid., pp. 269, 271.

[25]Jean-André Fieschi and A.-S. Labarth, "Nouvel
entretien avec Georges Franju," Cahiers du Cinéma
149 (1963), 10.

[26]Vialle, Georges Franju, p. 128.

[27]Bultmann, Primitive Christianity, p. 165.

[28]Fieschi, "Nouvel entretien," p. 15; cf. R.
Borde, "Georges Franju et le réalisme poétique,"
Image et Son 146 (1961), 10.

7

ONE FLEW OVER THE CUCKOO'S NEST

AND THE MYTH OF THE FISHER KING

Margaret J. Yonce

Perhaps no myth is more congenial to the temper of our age, no myth more potentially powerful, no myth more capable of stimulating the creative process than that of the Fisher King. The maimed and impotent king who rules over a sterile and empty wasteland seems a proper symbol for a civilization balanced on the brink of nuclear catastrophe or ecological suicide, and his restoration to health and fertility generates at least the hope that our own society can regain its health before we become the final wasteland. Certainly, T. S. Eliot sensed this when he used the myth of the Fisher King as the central underlying image in The Waste Land, though he undoubtedly was more concerned with spiritual than with physical drought. Perhaps Jessie Weston (whose study of the Grail Quest in From Ritual to Romance gave Eliot his "plan and a good deal of the incidental symbolism"[1] for his poem) is correct when she asserts that the story "is a living force, [that] will never die; [that] it may indeed sink out of sight, and, for centuries even, disappear . . . but it will rise to the surface again, and become once more a theme of vital inspiration."[2] At any rate, whether as a result of Eliot's epoch-defining poem or because of its own inherent power and vitality, the story of the Fisher King has become, if not

a myth for all seasons, at least a myth for our
season.

One novelist who has found such a source for
inspiration and creative energy in the Fisher King
story is Ken Kesey, whose popular novel One Flew
Over the Cuckoo's Nest (1962) employs the myth as an
indwelling metaphor that adds dimension and depth to
a story at times bordering on the simplistic and
superficial. Though I do not wish here to get into
the problem of intent, I think it safe to assume
that Kesey was familiar with the Fisher King story,
probably from The Waste Land and perhaps from Miss
Weston's book or other studies of the myth, and that
he used it in much the same way Eliot had used it in
The Waste Land, to provide a plan and much of the
symbolism for his novel.

Indeed, a careful investigation of Kesey's novel
reveals numerous parallels of a fairly precise
nature which, whether accidental or intentional, are
certainly fortunate and can lead to a deeper understanding and appreciation of the novel. On the
other hand, let me state at the outset that there
are many aspects of the Fisher King/Grail Quest
(including some quite important elements) for which
there are no obvious parallels in One Flew Over the
Cuckoo's Nest. There are also several points at
which Kesey diverges from or alters the myth. And
while I do not wish to stretch the fabric of my
argument beyond what it will support, I would con-
jecture that the omissions and alterations are intentional, that what is changed or left out is perhaps
as significant as what is included.

Before discussing the parallels in One Flew Over
the Cuckoo's Nest, perhaps it would be advantageous
to rehearse in its brief outlines the story of the
Fisher King as presented by Miss Weston. Although,
as we shall see, the myth appeared in several different forms in various Grail manuscripts, the basic
legend is as follows: On the banks of a river in
the midst of a barren land stands a castle ruled
over by a maimed and impotent king known as the
Fisher King. In some mysterious fashion, the condition of the kingdom is connected with the health of
the ruler; until he is cured, his land will remain
under the curse. The curse will be removed only by
the intercession of a knight courageous enough to
make his way to the Fisher King's domain and bold

enough to ask the meaning of various objects shown
to him. The task of the Grail Knight, which is
known as the "Freeing of the Waters," restores both
king and country to vigor and fertility.

The most obvious candidate for the role of Fisher
King in One Flew Over the Cuckoo's Nest is Chief
Bromden, the six-foot-seven-inch Columbia Gorge
Indian who has successfully feigned deafness and
muteness for years as protection against the "Combine." His tribe, which has been forced off its
lands by a government-built hydroelectric project,
had traditionally sustained itself by fishing for
salmon on the falls of the Columbia River. As one
of the inmates of the asylum explains, Bromden is
the son of the "tribal leader, hence this fellow's
title, 'Chief.'"[3] Thus Chief Bromden is literally
both a "fisher" and a "king." That he is "maimed"
goes without saying, though his infirmity is mental
or spiritual rather than physical. He wanders in a
schizophrenic fog, trying to hide from the attend-
ants and believing himself to be small and weak.

If we pursue this comparison further, we find
that the parallels extend below the surface level
of similarity. Miss Weston points out that in some
versions of the legend we have not one but two
Fisher Kings, one suffering the effects of a wound
and the other--his father or in some texts his
grandfather--suffering the infirmities of old age.
Similarly, Chief Bromden's father, whom we see only
through flashes of his son's memory, was once a
strong and hearty man known as "Tee Ah Milatoona,"
"The-Pine-That-Stands-Tallest-on-the-Mountain"
(p. 186). His will and his sight were gradually
destroyed by his white town wife, cheap cactus
liquor, and the encroachment of the establishment.
Memories of his father continue to haunt Chief
Bromden, as when he recalls his father's death: "the
last I see him he's blind in the cedars from drink-
ing and every time I see him put the bottle to his
mouth he don't suck out of it, it sucks out of him
until he's shrunk so wrinkled and yellow even the
dogs don't know him, and we had to cart him out of
the cedars, in a pickup, to a place in Portland, to
die" (p. 188). Indeed, Chief Bromden's illness can
be traced to his recognition of his father's loss of
power and physical deterioration. Moreover, the
decline of the tribe as a whole is linked to the

deterioration of the Chief. Once Chief Tee Ah
Milatoona is pressured into selling the tribe's
land for the hydroelectric dam, the Indians disperse,
some to working on the building of the dam itself,
some to the towns and cities where a few prosper but
many, like the Chief, drift into aimlessness, idle-
ness, drunkenness, and loss of vitality. Thus, in a
very real sense, the health of the land and the
people depends upon the health of the ruler. Ironi-
cally, the building of the dam for the power plant
deprives the Indians of their source of power; it is
a literal stoppage of the waters, which the Grail
Knight symbolically must free.

We may also find significant parallels in the
nature of the infirmities that afflict Chief Bromden
and his father. In most versions of the myth, the
Fisher King is said to be suffering from a wound in
the thigh or the loins, which, as Miss Weston points
out, is a euphemism for impotence and loss of virility, perhaps even originally castration. While we
do not know whether Chief Bromden is sexually
impotent (there is virtually no occasion to discover
or test his virility), it is abundantly clear that
he is impotent in other ways; he has indeed lost his
power. He sees himself as small, weak, ineffectual.
When McMurphy tells him, "You stand a head taller'n
any man on the ward. There ain't a man here you
couldn't turn every way but loose . . . ," he replies, "No. I'm way too little. I used to be big,
but not no more. You're twice the size of me"
(p. 186). Also, according to Miss Weston, in one
version of the Grail legend the host of the castle
"is really dead, and only compelled to retain the
semblance of life till the task of the Quester be
achieved" (pp. 115-116). This state of death-in-
life is certainly an accurate metaphor for the
Chief's condition as well as one of the predominant
wasteland motifs of the novel.

If we pursue this line of investigation further
we inevitably must consider the theme of castration
in the novel. Instances of this motif abound: the
Big Nurse is appropriately called a "ball cutter";
lobotomy is termed "frontal lobe castration"; and
Chief Bromden recalls the incident in which one of
the patients, Old Rawler, "cut both nuts off and
bled to death, sitting right on the can in the
latrine, half a dozen people in there with him

didn't know it till he fell off to the floor, dead"
(p. 115). In terms of the meaning of the novel this
emphasis on castration, of course, illustrates the
debilitating effect of the institution, the Establishment, the "Combine," its power to rob the individual of his manhood. Symbolically, it represents
the sterility of the wasteland world, its barren-
ness, its loss of vitality and fecundity. On the
mythic level it perhaps harkens back to the priests
of Attis, who practiced ritual self-mutilation in
emulation of their god, who was said to have castrated himself and bled to death under a pine tree.[4]
As Miss Weston's study makes clear, the vegetation
cults such as those of Attis, Adonis, Tammuz, and
Mithra are the origin of the rituals, myths, and
symbols carried over into the Grail Romances. Thus
the maiming attributed to the Fisher King was in
reality the vestiges of self-mutilation practiced
by the priests of Attis. It may be pushing the
parallel too far, but it is interesting to speculate
that the association of Chief Bromden's father,
Tee Ah Milatoona, with the pine tree (sacred to
Attis) and his blindness (a conventional Freudian
symbol for castration) also equate him with the
Attis cult.

Having thus established Chief Bromden as the
wounded Fisher King, we may now turn our attention
to the bold knight whose endurance and questioning
restore health to the Fisher King and vitality to
his lands and people. This quester in One Flew Over
the Cuckoo's Nest is, of course, Randle Patrick
McMurphy, the brawling, lusty, card-playing rowdy
whose appearance initiates profound changes in the
neat, ordered, sterile routine of the mental ward.
Though a far cry from the medieval Grail Knight of
legend, McMurphy nevertheless performs the same
service--the eventual restoration of the Fisher
King and his land. Like Gawain and Percival before
him, McMurphy performs his task by asking questions.
His questions do not, however, concern the meaning
of various mystical symbols shown to him; rather;
they are seemingly innocent and mundane inquiries:
why does the toothpaste have to be locked up and
dispensed at regulated times; why must the television set be turned on only at certain hours and
why can't an exception be made for the World Series;
why do the inmates themselves allow Nurse Ratched

and her staff to dominate and demean them? In fact,
McMurphy questions and eventually challenges virtually every facet of the institution's system,
procedure, and authority. His presence and attitude
finally free at least some of the inmates--including
Chief Bromden--from the power of the Combine.

Questioning is not, however, the only task which
McMurphy performs. He endures the terrors of the
Chapel Perilous, in this case the mental institution
itself, and particularly the Shock Shop, where he is
subjected to the "therapy" of repeated electroshock
treatment until Nurse Ratched decides he is more of
a threat as a legend than as a reality and relents.
He undertakes a "test of strength"--the lifting of
the massive control panel in the hydrotherapy room;
and though he fails to raise the instrument, his
valiant effort sufficiently impresses the other
inmates to effect a change in their attitudes.
Where they had been passive and submissive, they
now assert their own desires and for the first time
turn against the Big Nurse by voting to be allowed
to watch the World Series. In the atmosphere of
sterility and sexual deprivation fostered by Nurse
Ratched and the institution, McMurphy is a virile
and potent force, constantly affirming his own
"whambam" and introducing into the sexual vacuum of
the ward pornographic playing cards and Portland
prostitutes. Perhaps most important, he engages in
single combat with Nurse Ratched, and though he
ultimately goes down in defeat, her hold over the
ward appears weakened if not finally broken. The
Grail Knight in the Perilous Chapel was confronted
by a huge and loathsome black hand which threatened
life and limb and which he fought against and
wounded; Randle Patrick McMurphy confronts Nurse
Ratched, a terror of starched whiteness, does battle
with, and at least diminishes his foe.

Two episodes in the novel are particularly significant for our investigation: the deep sea fishing
expedition and the wild party which marks both
McMurphy's triumph and his defeat. The fishing trip
itself is an exercise in restoring the inmates'
health. For many of them it is the first contact
with the outside world in years, and under
McMurphy's leadership they regain a portion of their
lost self-confidence, self-esteem, and self-control.
The desire to go on the trip prompts Chief Bromden

to break his long self-imposed silence and speak.
His return to health can be gauged by his renewed
sense of identity and power. When the aids put a
broom in his hands on the morning of the trip, he
refuses it, thinking, "A man goin' fishing with
two whores from Portland don't have to take that
crap" (p. 191).

It may be well to pause for a moment to examine
two important symbols: bird and fish. Both creatures appear so frequently in the novel that they
virtually demand that we view them symbolically.
Here again, I believe, Miss Weston provides the
clue: quoting Cumont she states, "'Two animals were
held in general reverence [by pagan fertility
cults], namely, Dove and Fish'" (p. 133), and she
goes on to add that the inclusion of dove and fish
in the iconography of the Grail Romances is undoubtedly a vestige of their former signification. They
are, she asserts, "life symbols of immemorial
antiquity" (p. 135), and "it was the prolific nature
of the Fish, a feature which it shares in common
with the Dove" (p. 135) which inspired their adop-
tion as symbols of fertility. Of the many references to both fish and birds that abound in the
novel, we may single out for illustration one where
the two appear together. Significantly, it occurs
during the fishing expedition and marks the moment
when the Chief catches his salmon:

> George sang out for us to look up ahead,
> that here come just what we been looking for.
> I leaned around to look, but all I saw was a
> big drifting log and those black seagulls
> circling and diving around the log, like
> black leaves caught up in a dust devil.
> George speeded up some, heading into the
> place where the birds circled, and the speed
> of the boat dragged my line until I couldn't
> see how you'd be able to tell if you did get
> a bite.
>
> "Those fellas, those cormorants, they go
> after a school of <u>candle</u> fishes," George told
> us as he drove. "Little white fishes the
> size of your finger. You dry them and they
> burn joost like a candle. They are <u>food</u>
> fish, chum fish. And you bet where there's

a big school of them candle fish you find the
silver salmon feeding."
    He drove into the birds, missing the float-
ing log, and suddenly all around me the smooth
slopes of chrome were shattered by diving
birds and churning minnows, and the sleek
silver-blue torpedo backs of the salmon
slicing through it all. (pp. 209-10)

The sexual overtones of the fishing trip are perhaps
too readily apparent. Not only the presence on
board of the little whore Candy and her amatory
exploits in the ship's cabin with McMurphy, but also
the phallic implications of the fishing poles and
the frequent admonitions by the captain to "Keep the
tip up!" (p. 210) underscore the expedition's function of restoring virility and potency to the
sexually wasted inmates. When they return to shore,
covered with fish blood and silver scales, they are
the newly baptized initiates in the cult of fertility, ready now to partake of the final mystery.
    The climax of the novel--the wild party which
breaks down the patients' last remaining restraints
--also serves an important mythic function. The
many critics who have noted the analogies to
Christian myth in One Flew Over the Cuckoo's Nest
have been quick to point out that the party episode
parallels Christ's Last Supper. Though they are
indeed correct, I believe that the episode contains
another parallel to a ritual which antedates the
Christian Eucharist and indeed gave to it some of
its features. I am referring, of course, to the
initiation rituals of the various vegetation deities, the cults of Attis, Adonis, Tammuz, Osiris,
and Mithra. The party re-enacts the life ritual,
the revelation to the initiate of the secrets of
life and death. The vegetation cults, Miss Weston
notes, had both an exoteric and an esoteric phase.
Only a select few were admitted to the secret,
inner rites where the central mystery was revealed.
Likewise, the party is a secret affair in which
only a few of the inmates--those who are ready for
independent selfhood--participate. Not even all
of the twelve "disciples" who followed McMurphy on
the fishing trip take part in the party. The cele-
brants share in a communal meal of sorts, substituting pot, pills, and vodka-laced cough syrup for

the sacramental meal of fish, bread, and wine par-
taken of by worshippers of the mystery cults and
early Christians alike. It is tempting to see in
the wild abandon of the party a re-enactment of the
feast of <u>Hilaria</u>, or Festival of Joy, which accompanied the celebration of Attis' rebirth. According
to Frazer, the divinity's resurrection "was celebrated with a wild outburst of glee. . . . A universal licence prevailed. Every man might say and do
what he pleased. . . . No dignity was too high or
too sacred for the humblest citizen to assume with
impunity."[5] This is precisely the spirit which
characterizes the hilarity of McMurphy's party. As
Chief Bromden relates, "we laughed till we were
rolling about the couches and chairs, choking and
teary eyed. . . . I was drunk, actually drunk, glow-
ing and grinning and staggering drunk for the first
time since the Army, drunk along with half a dozen
other guys and a couple of girls--right on the Big
Nurse's ward!" (pp. 233-35).

The primary purpose of the party on both literal
and mythic levels is the initiation of Billy Bibbit
into the mystery of sex. Just as the mystery of
generation was at the heart of the life cults, so
Billy must achieve sexual experience before he can
hope to be free and whole. Yet here, of course, is
where McMurphy's "cure" fails. Nurse Ratched's
threat to tell Billy's mother after she discovers
him with the prostitute destroys his tenuous selfhood and causes him to commit suicide. Indeed,
looked at from a different angle, the whole party
episode becomes a reversal of the mystery rites.
Where the vegetation celebrations began with lamen-
tations for the slain god but ended with jubilation
at his rebirth, McMurphy's party begins in hilarity
and ends in tragedy. Where the worshipper of Attis
was baptized in blood as a symbol of rebirth,
Billy's slashed throat bathes him in blood and marks
his death.

The conclusion of the novel makes the most dramatic reversal and alteration of the Fisher King myth.
In no version of the Grail Romances does the quester
himself die or fall under the curse. He may fail
to ask the proper questions that would restore the
Fisher King's health, but his failure does not
threaten his own life. Yet this is precisely what
happens in Kesey's novel: McMurphy, the Grail

Knight, and Chief Bromden, the Fisher King, exchange roles. Chief Bromden, restored to full vigor and "size," heaves the control panel that McMurphy had failed to lift through the window and escapes, symbolically "Freeing the Waters": "The glass splashed out in the moon, like a bright cold water baptizing the sleeping earth" (pp. 271-72). There is an indication that he will return to his home on the Columbia River and rejoin his people, who also seem to have regained their health; "I've even heard," he says, "that some of the tribe have took to building their old ramshackle wood scaffolding all over that big million-dollar hydroelectric dam, and are spearing salmon in the spillway" (p. 272). McMurphy, however, fallen under the curse of the Establishment, symbolically castrated by the frontal lobotomy, seems doomed to a wasteland death-in-life existence until the Chief frees him by mercifully suffocating him with a pillow. Thus the myth of the Fisher King merges with the myth of the scapegoat-savior in which the death of the sacrificial victim is required to release others to life. In the modern wasteland, it seems, even the greatest sacrifices achieve only partial victories. The king must die, but his death does not assure the restoration or rejuvenation of his people.

NOTES

[1] T. S. Eliot, "Notes on 'The Waste Land,'" The Waste Land and Other Poems (New York: Harcourt, Brace & World, Inc., 1934), p. 47.

[2] Jessie L. Weston, From Ritual to Romance (Garden City, New York: Doubleday Anchor Books, 1957), p. 188. Subsequent references to this edition will appear parenthetically within the text.

[3] Ken Kesey, One Flew Over the Cuckoo's Nest (New York: Viking Press, 1962), p. 27. Subsequent references to this edition will appear parenthetically within the text.

[4]Sir James G. Frazer, The New Golden Bough, ed. Theodore H. Gaster (New York: Mentor Books, 1964), pp. 370-73.

[5]Frazer, p. 373.

8

LANDSCAPE VIEWED AND RE-VIEWED:

ANTONIONI'S THE PASSENGER

Barbara Hodgdon

"The visual arts," said Bernard Berenson, "are a compromise between what we see and what we know."[1] I know of no better way to characterize the multiple levels of experience--the creative experience of the film artist, the experience of his central charac- ter, David Locke, and the viewing experience of the spectator--offered by Antonioni's The Passenger.[2]
On the narrative level the film explores the theme of the man who moves into another man's life, or into his role, in an attempt to escape his own life and to find freedom. David Locke (Jack Nicholson), a journalist, is trying to make a tele- vision film about a guerilla movement in Northern Africa. Frustrated by his attempts to contact the guerillas, Locke returns to his hotel and discovers that David Robertson, a traveler he has met briefly, has died of a heart attack. By switching passport photographs and changing clothes with the dead man, Locke trades identities with Robertson and sets off rather casually to follow the dead man's itinerary. Soon Locke discovers that Robertson was a highly paid gunrunner who was to supply arms to Achebe, the leader of the guerilla movement Locke had been trying to film.
Simultaneously, Locke's wife, Rachel, and his television producer, Martin Knight, begin to search

for Robertson (not knowing that Locke has changed
places with him) because he was presumably the last
person to see Locke alive. But when Rachel finds
the changed photograph in Locke's passport, the
pursuit grows more frantic. Achebe is captured by
the secret police, who are also following Rachel,
assuming that she will lead them to the man they
think is Robertson.

In order to elude Martin Knight and his wife,
Locke seeks the aid of a Girl (Maria Schneider), who
joins him in his flight. She tries to convince him
of a rationale for following Robertson's appointed
rounds. Finally everyone--police, Rachel, Achebe's
kidnappers--catches up with Locke, and we assume
that the kidnappers, who arrive first, kill Locke,
thinking he is Robertson.

However confusing this narrative may seem at
times, Antonioni's film contains no totally novel
situations. The elements are familiar, not only
because we have seen them in other Antonioni films
(Il Grido, Una Cronaca d'un Amore, L'Eclisse, Blow-
Up) but because the film scenario touches upon--and
refashions--the dimensions of the model existential
"myth": the story of a man who rejects his profes-
sion, his past, and the historical past, moves
through moments of despair as he seeks commitment,
and finally sees himself as a self-contained unit.

After viewing the film, we can recognize the
outlines of this narrative territory; while we view
the film, however, what we seek to know is often
held in suspension by the images Antonioni chooses
to let us see.

The opening sequence, which shows Locke's several
attempts to contact the guerillas, immediately sets
up a dialectic between seeing and knowing and establishes "not knowing" as a key ingredient in the
film. We see Locke approach the natives and ask
(in nonsyntactic French) for directions. He re-
ceives no answers; he is waved away. If there are
ambiguities for Locke, these are enhanced for the
spectator. Who is this man? What does he do? What
is he looking for? Are the others hostile or merely
indifferent? Why? Locke returns to his Land Rover
and finds a boy in the passenger seat; they drive
off; the boy signals Locke to stop, gets out, and
walks away. Alone, Locke pauses in front of the
car to watch a man on a camel cross the desert

landscape, moving slowly from left to right. Independently, the camera moves in the opposite direction: the man is gone. After a bit, Locke and a
guide climb a hill, moving with difficulty through
a rock-strewn landscape. Suddenly the guide pushes
Locke down behind a rock. There seems to be no
reason to hide, and then we see a camel train of
armed men. When the men have passed, Locke's guide
has disappeared. Locke dismisses the incident with
a pass of his hand, a gesture that will be repeated
and exaggerated later in the film. His Land Rover
moves swiftly across the desert and up a hill; stuck
in the sand, its wheels spin. Locke tries to dig
it out but finally falls to his knees exclaiming:
"All right--I don't care!" Arbitrarily, the camera
tracks to empty desert, sky leveling the top of the
frame. The sound of rushing wind comes from off-
screen. Cut to a long shot of Locke, exhausted,
framed between buildings as he enters a town.

These moments, characterized by "lifts" of time,
do not show the whole of Locke's search. Antonioni's
camera isolates certain moments of his character's
narrative progress, a strategy that increases the
mysteriousness of Locke's situation. As spectators,
we receive information about Locke's situation at
the same time that he does, so that we share his
non-knowing point of view. This is one kind of
image, one way of seeing, which I will call a narrative image. But there are other kinds of images,
those of Antonioni's independent camera--long
panning shots of desert landscape, deliberate,
painterly moments that are not prompted by Locke's
glance and that reveal nothing except the natural
counterpointing of brown earth and brilliantly blue
sky. And both narrative and landscape images are
flooded by flat, blinding light--a device that lures
us into assuming that we see clearly, that we understand.

This clarity is, however, something of a hoax.
At this point, as elsewhere in the film, the only
thing that is quite clearly understood is the land-
scape--as seen through the assertive eye of the
camera. Often, the expressiveness of these shots
rests upon their quite literal silence as images:
the landscapes seem to look at us as much as we are
asked to look at them. A usual set-up (and this is
an established commonplace of Antonioni's cinematic

technique) shows us a long shot of landscape; a
figure entering the landscape; a closeup or mid-
closeup of the figure within the landscape; a shot
of the landscape without the figure. The relationship between figure and ground triggers a way of
seeing which suggests that although the human
presence may become, for a moment, a part of a
landscape, it echoes upon it only briefly before it
withdraws, leaving the landscape unchanged. Locke
encounters the landscape; we encounter the landscape: yet neither pattern of images reveals what
it is that causes him--or us--to be there. These
independent images heighten the mystery for the
viewer. They are so polished and so refined, and
there is such an echoed deliberation in their
design, that the eye loses them. Paradoxically,
they seem to be read easily, yet they refuse explanation. They commit us to the film in a way
distinct from our narrative involvement, yet they
also allow us to remain apart from it, forcing us
to find meaning from a distanced perspective. This
remote contact with many of the film's images--even
within the narrative images, we rarely see a close
focus on faces as registers of feelings and meanings
--prompts us to watch more purposefully.

The film moves in a leisurely fashion through its
early sequences: here, Antonioni establishes color
as a suggestive transitional device, linking large
perceptible areas of the film, triggering and
heightening emotional auras for his characters and
for the viewer. Unmodulated stretches of sand
tones, punctuated by blues, lead us into the film;
blue and white, set off by yellow accents, dominate
the moments when Locke takes over Robertson's
identity--by putting on Robertson's blue jacket,
which we never see again. And blue further defines
and summarizes Locke's most ecstatic release into
freedom, which comes when he leans out from a cable
car in Barcelona, his arms spread like wings (interestingly, the gesture is the natural exaggerated
extension of that earlier shrug of shoulder and hand
registering indifference or helplessness). Far
below him the blue of the water echoes his own
repose. Although he is moving, and although we see
the ripples on the water, the effect of the shot is
to suspend him within that moment of space--it is
at once the most mobile and the most static moment

in the film--and this is partly because for once he
and his landscape seem to be completely harmonious.

This sense of natural harmony, appearing only in
the central spaces of the film, where the film's
ability to shift time and locale reflects Locke's
freedom and his ability to move through space, is
reinforced by the use of greens and browns, by a
speeded-up film rhythm, and by shots of deepened
visual richness and complexity. Yet even the most
complex backgrounds are made architectonically alert
by Antonioni's strict compositional eye. A sense
of "desert-ness" prevails, even in the city-scapes
--we see it in the angularity of the Bloomsbury
apartment block where Locke first sees the Girl; in
the twisting, stylized bleakness of the Gaudi
building where Locke meets the Girl a second time
and asks her for help; in the planes and angles of
the Plaza de la Iglesia, where Locke waits to ren-
dezvous with the mysterious Daisy. None of these
deserts gives Locke a place to hide; increasingly,
we see him trapped, either within an architectural
frame or within the frame of the film.

Although Antonioni's cadenced, meditative cinematic style does distance us from the film, it is
not, ultimately, a way to withhold knowing. Be-
sides the two types of images--narrative and inde-
pendent--already described, Antonioni also selects
a third way of seeing, one which allows us to "re-
see" Locke--through flashbacks, in a prophetic
sequence documenting Achebe's arrest and beating;
in moments seen from Rachel's point of view as she
attempts to "reinvent" her husband; and through
media images which Locke himself has generated.
Overall, the film sets up a fluid exchange among
these three kinds of images, so that the present,
the memory of the past, others' points of view, and
the visual commentary of Antonioni's apparently
disinterested camera gain significance through juxtaposition.

When their linkages are considered as a "mini-
film" within the larger structure, the film clips
made by Locke offer an oblique commentary on knowing, on what Antonioni calls "the myth of objectivity."[3] The first of them, Locke's filmed obituary, places his past--from the rather artificially
banal perspective of Martin Knight and his col-
leagues. "He had a talent for observation," Knight

says. "He had a sense of detachment. . . . He was searching for objectivity. . . . He was a human-ist."[4] Rachel watches the talk show on a TV set; Locke listens outside the door. The event initiates her curiosity about defining Locke; Locke himself crosses the street, glances at his (Robertson's) airline ticket, and leaves.

In the next of these images, which we see on a movieola before the focus widens to full-screen, Locke is interviewing the African president. His questions receive stock answers--responses that reveal nothing. The camera cuts away to Rachel and Martin in the studio and then returns to a full-screen image of the interview and its complete surroundings from Rachel's point of view. She accuses Locke of being involved in real situations without having real dialogue, of allowing the president to lie. Neutrality, not objectivity, seems to be his forte. Achebe's arrest and beating, recorded by the omniscient camera, follow these images. Objective? Yes--and no. Neutral? Hardly, for the events foreshadow Locke's own end. Now we return to Locke's story: we see him briefly in a bar in Munich, then in the cable car, and next in the Umbraculo, where he meets an old man who asks if Locke wants to hear his life story. But these sequences, revealing Locke's most serene moments, are quickly destroyed. The greens of the trees in the shaded arbor give way to the greenish tint of the next shots: full-screen newsreel footage of the military execution of three Africans on a beach. As he is shot, one of the men echoes Locke's expressive shrug of hand and arm. Cut to shots of Rachel and Martin, obviously disturbed, watching the film on a movieola. They make no comment. Yet the images shock us, as they may have shocked Locke, even momentarily, out of his neutrality.

In the last media image, the witchdoctor Locke is interviewing says, "There are perfectly satisfactory answers to all your questions. . . . But I don't think you understand how little you would learn from them. . . . Your questions are much more revealing about yourself than my answers would be about me." Suddenly he turns the camera on Locke. "Now," he says, "we can have an interview." We see Locke's intent, unspeaking face; he makes his characteristic gesture of resignation--a shrug with his hands. In

the studio, Martin Knight comments, "Toward the end
he seems to have gone off onto a track of his own."

However disjunctive, the progression here is one
that details Locke's unhinging--from the ordered
obituary that gives the illusion of all-knowing
objectivity, through several comments on Locke as
an onlooker, to seeing Locke as a passive, hesitant
participant, trapped by his own game.

In spite of Locke's activity during the escape
and chase narrative moments of the film, his character has a peculiar stasis, giving us the sense that
he is locked--the pun is intentional--into a way of
seeing. The image structure of the film accentuates
Locke's inability to free himself from particular
visions by repeating certain images--Robertson's
hotel room is a mirror image of Locke's; electric
wires leading nowhere and the lazy movement of fans
circling reoccur in different places; flies and
flower petals become matched cues for unleashing
Locke's emotions; the old man in the Umbraculo is
re-seen, sitting outside the room where Locke dies
in the final moments of the film. There is a
pellucid suggestiveness about these re-visions--as
though Antonioni is saying that man perceives only
so many images and that, in his visual life, these
images tend to recur. Their duration may alter, and
the man's point of view may change slightly--in
Locke's case this shift moves toward seeing with
increased disgust--but both what we see, as well as
our ways of seeing, remain fairly stable.

Within its last sequences, as color and complexity gradually wash out of the film, turning it
nearly "white" in the final moments, The Passenger
turns firmly to refocus upon the question of seeing.

We are in the Hotel de la Gloria, where Locke
has come, alone, to the last destination on
Robertson's itinerary. When he registers, he discovers that the Girl is there, even though he has
sent her away. Locke opens the door to the Girl's
room and we see her, reflected in a mirror, standing
at the window. "What can you see?" Locke asks. She
describes a scene: "A little boy, and an old woman,
having an argument--about which way to go. . . . A
man scratching his leg. A shutter closing. A kid
and dust. It's very dusty." Is the moment real or
imagined? We never know. Locke's sightlines focus
on the Girl; we see her mirror image; she sees

something unseen by Locke, by us. Locke's imagination, as well as his literal vision, seem to have
failed.

Of the images that follow, one hauntingly expresses, for me, this failure of Locke's imagination: it is a shot of the picture hanging over the
bed in the room where he dies. This sequence leads
up to it: in a monumental two-shot closeup, Locke
and the Girl stare out at us from the sides of the
screen, as though looking at nothing. Locke tells
the Girl of a man who was blind, and who, when he
was nearly forty, got his sight back. "At first
he was elated. . . . Then everything started to
change; . . . the world was much poorer than he
had imagined. . . . No one had ever told him how
much dirt there was, how much ugliness." (Here,
Locke's words reflect his own experience as well as
the re-imaging process of the film.) Locke continues: "He started to live in the dark; . . . after
three years he killed himself." Locke and the Girl
embrace. Independently, the camera moves up an
electrical wire to the picture. It is, of course,
a landscape--an evocative, sentimentally Byronic
landscape of a castle tower, a river and woods, a
beautifully clouded sky. Like other landscapes in
the film, it awaits an inhabitant. For a moment
the camera realizes the freedom that Locke cannot.

Having brushed this image across the screen,
Antonioni quickly returns to the narrative. "What
the hell are you doing here with me?" asks Locke.
The Girl leaves; we see Locke's face; he opens the
window, lights a cigarette, and lies down on the
bed. We are set up for the last shot.

At the end of L'Eclisse Antonioni played with
seven minutes of reel time, containing fifty-eight
shots, reviewing people and objects seen by Piero
and Vittoria when they met. We are reminded of the
leading characters by shots of people who, seen
from the back or from a distance, resemble them.
But when the camera moves in to look more closely,
the faces are not theirs. Gradually the sequence
builds a sense of emptiness and coldness--it ends
with the coming of night over the building site;
the lovers never meet. We are invited to generalize
that solitude is man's usual state.

In The Passenger Antonioni again uses seven
minutes of reel time--this time all within one shot

--to complete his film. As in L'Eclisse the content
of the images echoes previous moments of the film.
But Antonioni has gone beyond the "existential" ending of L'Eclisse to give us a different generaliza-
tion, a newfound conclusion.

We leave Locke's figure, stretched out on the bed
in the Hotel de la Gloria. Again autonomous, the
tracking camera moves slowly outside the window to
look at the incidental qualities of figure/ground
relationships--an old man, a child, the Girl, a
moving vehicle, all carefully choreographed echoes
of earlier shots--before rejoining the narrative
briefly to document the discovery of Locke's body.
Rachel admits, "I never knew him." But the Girl,
when asked "Do you know him?," replies "Yes." Yet
we have seen only fragments of this knowing. Locke
remains a mystery--to himself, to us. He ends in
repose, contained, closed off. His dilemma is,
however, resolved by Antonioni's omniscient camera,
which moves away from the images of narrative
closure to examine--landscape: the facade of the
Hotel de la Gloria, where the sun is setting. The
camera allows us, as viewers, to end in, first,
freedom, and then repose. It can show Locke and
document his story and, within that story, his
moments of found freedom--his exultant reach over
the water, his flight from the past in a car--but
it can also push beyond his ending to show the twi-
light calm of the Hotel de la Gloria. Just as the
witchdoctor turned the camera on Locke, so does the
final image of the film turn back to show us where
we have been. It is our seeing, not Locke's, that
completes the series of images comprising and surrounding his life. The closure effected by the
omniscient camera provides an enigmatic compromise
between seeing and knowing: man, and whatever he
sees or does not see, gives way to landscape--a
landscape that both places us apart from and invites
us into a mysteriously suggested glory.

                         NOTES

[1]Bernard Berenson, Seeing and Knowing (London:
Chapman and Hall, 1953), p. 37.

[2]I am indebted to my colleague, Richard Abel, for suggestions and comments that helped to shape my thinking and writing about Antonioni's film.

[3]In an article by Richard F. Shepard, "Antonioni Pauses Here in His Search," New York Times, 1975, reprinted in Mark Peploe, Peter Wollen, and Michelangelo Antonioni, The Passenger (New York: Grove Press, Inc., 1975), pp. 189-92.

[4]All quotes are from the published version of the filmscript: Mark Peploe, Peter Wollen, and Michelangelo Antonioni, The Passenger (New York: Grove Press, Inc., 1975).

9

THE ANTICHRIST-FIGURE IN THREE

LATIN AMERICAN NOVELS

William L. Siemens

One is inclined to suspect that all notable novels represent the stirrings of restless giants, and an evident corollary is that in times of genuine socio-political turmoil the novel will strongly reflect an apocalyptic consciousness. In Latin America both of these statements hold true, for in the wrenching upheavals characteristic of nearly all those nations in recent years—not to say throughout their entire history—the novelist has been engaged in an attempt to shape the chaos which often appears to constitute his only raw material into some sort of manageable order.

In the attempt he has tended to make full use of the type of apocalyptic imagery most accessible to him and most comprehensible to his readers—the biblical. One curious point is that this body of imagery is generally poured into some rather unbiblical forms. For example, whereas the Book of Revelation is solidly committed to what is at least fundamentally a linear concept of time, in which all the disorder that the Beast and his allies can bring about is ultimately crushed in a once-for-all consummation, the new novel which uses much of the same symbolism tends to function within the cyclical framework more characteristic of primitive thought.

So what we have is something of a hybrid, a novel
which reflects the author's perception of a world at
the end of one of the infinite series of cosmic
cycles, perhaps a victim of entropy and the resul-
tant chaos, and expectant of the coming of some sort
of new creation. Yet the novels appear by their
choice of imagery to fit within at least a vaguely
Catholic framework. Even in the case of One Hundred
Years of Solitude, in which García Márquez lays so
much stress upon the single cycle of one hundred
years, the point is that a family condemned to one
hundred years of solitude will receive no second
chance,[1] the implication being that normally there
is another cycle to be expected.

In either tradition the power to recreate the
cosmos, to reestablish order, is supposed to be
brought back by a hero-figure, an elect being who
has departed from the hopelessly entropic situation
prevailing in his world in order to penetrate to the
appropriate source of that power. And the simple
fact is that the most prominent hero within the
frame of reference of these authors is the Christ
of the gospels and tradition. While it would seem
simpler just to construct a generalized hero whose
description would match, for example, that of
Campbell's Hero with a Thousand Faces,[2] what we are
confronted with more often is a hero who appears in
greater or lesser measure to be either reproducing
or reversing the characteristics and exemplary acts
specifically of Jesus Christ.

It is precisely this ambivalence with regard to
reproducing or reversing those acts that makes an
explanation of the word "antichrist" necessary. The
term itself is derived from two of the Johannine
epistles of the New Testament, where it denotes any
person who attempts to lead Christians astray.
Later in church history it was applied to the first
Beast of the Apocalypse, a destructive being whose
purpose is directly to oppose that of Christ rather
than simply substituting for him. The original
meaning of the Greek preposition 'anti' is "opposite," and throughout the history of the church the
term "antichrist" has been used almost exclusively
with reference to an entity in direct opposition to
Christ and his church.

For the sake of the present investigation, however, it will be used in the broader sense of the

Johannine epistles, to designate any person who, by
positive or negative reference to the attributes and
deeds of Christ, stands in the latter's place. This
usage is justified by the fact that, according to
the Arndt and Gingrich lexicon, most generally the
preposition 'anti' is used in the New Testament "in
order to indicate that one person or thing is, or is
to be, replaced by another,"[3] which is a rather more
general meaning than the popular one presented
above.

There have also been eliminated from considera-
tion--more or less arbitrarily--all the novels of
dictatorship that have appeared in such striking,
and one might say alarming, profusion in the past
few years. I am referring to García Márquez'
Autumn of the Patriarch, Carpentier's Reasons of
State, Aguilera-Malta's The Kidnapping of the
General, and Roa Bastos' I the Supreme, all of which
present their own special sort of messianic figure,
the dictator who masks his obsession with the power
to oppress by presenting to the people an image of
himself as their savior.

It is, however, another novel by one of these
authors with which I want to begin, namely Aguilera-
Malta's Seven Moons and Seven Serpents.[4] In it the
previously mentioned apocalyptic conditions are
prevalent: the jungle town that serves as its
setting is described in terms of pristine newness,
as it appears to be emerging from chaos through
primordial unity into creative diversity. The
battle between good and evil is almost Manichaean
in its simplicity, and the basic struggle revolves
around a huge priest named Cándido, who, like
Voltaire's Candide, finds his naiveté and innocence
taking a bit of a beating in a primitive South
American paradise.

Closely associated with Cándido are a positive
figure and a negative one, which I feel must be
interpreted as something like projections of those
propensities as they exist within him. I am con-
vinced that they are to be taken in this way in
part because of the narrative technique of the book,
in which basic novelistic reality is often presented
as an alternative to what the reader comes to realize is merely the hallucination of a character. For
example, at the end of one chapter the narrator himself asks whether what he has just described really

took place or not (p. 120). Obviously it is
Aguilera-Malta's intention to keep his reader off
balance in this regard.

Another example is seen in the manner in which
Cándido acquires the large crucifix which I feel
serves as the embodiment of his Christlike qualities. It is presented to him by an anachronistic
pirate who throws both it and the priest overboard.
An indication of the way their relationship will go
is seen in the fact that Cándido merely flounders
around in the water until the Christ suggests that
he climb onto the cross and row them out: he is
made of wood, after all, which is both good news
and bad news in the water (p. 34). From that time
on the priest goes frequently to ask advice of the
Christ, who gives it in refreshingly practical
terms. And since he is unable to come down--except
on one occasion when he descends from the cross to
beat five would-be murderers with it (p. 119)--he
must use Cándido as his instrument for good.

I have indicated that 'anti' may mean "opposite,"
and in this world of elemental struggles the clergy-
man must put up with what Jung would call a projection of his shadow, in this case a character at the
opposite extreme from his Christ. This phenomenon
takes the form of one Colonel Candelario Mariscal
(the military ring of the name of the demonic figure
is no accident in an Ecuadorian novel). This being
is reputed to be the offspring of a liaison between
the devil and a crazy local mule named Pancha. That
name represents the feminine form of a nickname for
"Francisco," or Francis, and there is here a complex
joke involving St. Francis, who referred to his body
as "Brother Donkey," all of which makes me believe
that the entire affair represents Candido's mythifi-
cation of what the rumor about town indicates really
happened: that Cándido is the father of Candelario
and that it was the latter's all too human mother
who left the child on his doorstep.

Be that as it may, Candelario seems to assume the
proportions of the dragon known as Leviathan, which
represents primordial chaos in Levantine thought and
the enemy of Christ in Revelation 20 (though he is
not mentioned by name there), for he is regularly
metamorphosed into a crocodile and at one point goes
on a rampage of murder and general destruction. It
is in this context that his mock-Christlike quali-

ties emerge. He walks across the water to the boat
of a fisherman whom he is about to call as his captive "disciple"; he miraculously fills the boat with
fish (pp. 101-02); and later he is involved in an
incident in which his right-hand man cuts an ear off
another person (p. 108).

I have already alluded to the fact that Cándido's
relationship to the Christ of the crucifix and to
Candelario (note the three Cs) is that of a man to
his own capabilities for good and evil, respectively, as projected into other entities. Thus the
clearcut battle between these forces is understood
as actually taking place within one man. The
important point emerges at the conclusion of the
novel, when Candelario is suffering a terrible
(though also comical) punishment for his crimes and
the priest refuses to help him. The resolution
comes about only when the Christ-figure, who himself
has been partially burned by a church fire set by
the terrible son of the devil, insists that
Candelario must be helped simply because he is a
being in need of help and furthermore has suffered
enough. The book ends with Cándido rushing off to
his aid, as the author exalts both the psychological
principle of the acceptance of the shadow and the
theological one of agape, or undeserved love.

In Gabriel García Márquez' One Hundred Years of
Solitude there appears another colonel, one who also
represents an aspect of a major character, in this
case José Arcadio Buendía, but whose career is the
reverse of that of Candelario Mariscal. Whereas
Candelario sets out to bring death and destruction
to his society and is only too successful at it,
Aureliano Buendía is forced into action by the need
to put an end to the murders and general injustice
of the party in power and fails miserably in the
effort, losing all his thirty-two wars. I am
intrigued by García Márquez' seemingly ambivalent
attitude towards him: he treats him like a quixotic
idealist and, as such, as a figure to be both
laughed at and admired. There is, in fact, true
pathos in the passages in which, years after the
colonel's death, doubt is expressed concerning
whether he even existed.

Moreover, there is a curious passage which indicates quite clearly, I think, what attitude García
Márquez takes toward those who at least attempt to

bring down the oppressor. When Aureliano is confronted by the fact that he has been betrayed by
the leaders of his own party, who have gained power
in Bogotá by collaborating with the enemy, he
finally recognizes the futility of the struggle and
calls for a peace treaty. After the signing he
attempts to shoot himself through the heart. His
mother perceives the usual omens of a death in the
family: orange discs in the sky, a cooking pot full
of worms, and a vision of him accompanied by chant-
ing novices; but she wonders why she sees him with
his eyes open. As it turns out, he has missed his
heart--a failure again--and with a little mercuro-
chrome he recovers nicely. Still, he is considered
a martyr by the people (pp. 179-85).

Furthermore, now that the war is over Ursula
feels that she is free to repair the rundown house.
Not only does she thoroughly renovate it, but she
herself begins to dress in youthful clothes again
(pp. 184-85). Thus it is clear that in Aureliano
we have another antichrist-figure, but this time in
that other sense of a replacement for Christ rather
than one opposed to him, for Aureliano symbolically
dies on the day that he brings peace to the people
and then survives to witness the new life resulting
from that peace.

My point is underscored by the fact that all the
features I have mentioned are present at the conclusion of a chapter very near the center of the
novel. That chapter ends with a mention of New
Year's Day, and it is enlightening to see the
similarity between the opening of the next chapter
and the opening lines of the book. Chapter 1 begins,

> Many years later, as he faced the firing
> squad, Colonel Aureliano Buendía was to
> remember that distant afternoon when his
> father took him to discover ice. (p. 1)

The chapter at the center of the novel opens with
these words:

> Years later on his deathbed Aureliano Segundo
> would remember the rainy afternoon in June
> when he went into the bedroom to meet his
> first son. (p. 186)

This is completely analogous to what the author of
the Fourth Gospel does in opening his text with the
first words of the book of Genesis: "In the begin-
ing." That is, there has emerged a messianic figure
whose life, death, and resurrection have affected
the world so deeply that the event must be treated
as something of a new creation. Moreover, Aureliano
then spends the remainder of his life converting the
gold coins which have brought so much grief to the
world into little fishes; the fish, of course, is
recognizable as perhaps the earliest symbol of
Christ.

The irony of the case becomes evident when, years
after his death, a Conservative officer who has come
to kill the colonel's grandnephew for his protest
activities discovers the fishes and requests one as
a souvenir (pp. 316-17). García Márquez could have
made no more eloquent statement: as in the case of
Jesus Christ, the person is considered a hero even
by his mortal enemies while his principles are
rejected by nearly everyone in practice.

Another antichrist-figure, who is in some ways
even more fascinating than these two, is the one
called Bustrofedon, who appears in Guillermo Cabrera
Infante's Three Trapped Tigers.[5] His name is that
of a rhetorical device referring to the practice of
writing first in one direction and then the other,
and Cabrera Infante has referred to him as "the
two-way man."[6] The idea is that like Christ, he
serves as a link between the physical and metaphysical realms, and this is underscored by a casual
mention of the fact that he tends to hang around
O Street (which of course can be taken as "Zero
Street") (p. 139).

It is more significant, however, that Bustrofedon
is a person who "wanted to become language" (p.
318), since that point makes him a mirror-image of
Christ. That is, whereas Christ, according to the
Fourth Gospel, is the Word who became a human being
(John 1:14), Bustrofedon is a human being who at
least attempted to be the Word, and it seems clear
that the author intends us to understand that he has
attained his goal. Furthermore, while Adams was the
man who named things, Christ as the Second Adam
(I Corinthians 15) changed some names ("Simon" to
"Peter," for example). Bustrofedon, we are told,
"began to change the names of things" (p. 220), in

an apparent attempt to recreate his world by the
transformation of the language underlying it. More
specifically, he has his own section of the novel
("Rompecabeza," meaning "Head-cracker" or "Riddle"),
in which he engages in some rather complex metaphysical word play involving the concept of immortality, one feature of which deals with his attach-
ment of his name to that of each of the friends in
his inner circle, an act recalling the statement of
Christ in Revelation 3:12 concerning any faithful
disciple of his: "I will . . . write on him my new
name." It is appropriate as well that, as one
preoccupied with being the Word, instead of twelve
disciples he has a wheel composed of twelve letters
which, in various combinations, spell out twelve
words, most of which, at least, relate in some way
to the messianic theme (p. 214).

Eventually, however, it is his fate to die
suddenly, and an autopsy reveals that his death was
caused by a growth on his spinal column which put
pressure on his brain and made him engage in his
rather unrestrained word play (p. 222). To state
it another way, the same feature that set him apart
from other men both caused him to act as the creative Word and brought about his death, again as in
the case of Christ.

These figures and several others which could
have been mentioned suggest that an age of disinte-
gration into chaos is one into which the collective
unconscious seems to expect a hero-figure to spring
forth with the power of renewal. And, as I indicated at the beginning, in any literary tradition
steeped in the imagery of christendom, that hero-
figure tends to take on the proportions of an antichrist. The problem, in turn, is that one cannot
expect salvation from Antichrist. In the three
cases under consideration here the results are,
respectively, destruction followed by drastic punishment, failure resulting in disillusionment and
oblivion, and sudden death.

Even in the cases of Aureliano and Bustrofedon,
both of whom are presented in a comparatively positive light, there is no sign of the return from
Hades with the boon which signifies the regeneration
of life for the people. Much less is there the sort
of powerful impact upon the entire cosmos which
should be evident in the career of a character

possessing some of Christ's attributes. Thus that cosmos is doomed to proceed on its inexorably entropic way, seemingly without hope of any new surge of creative energy before it dies with the notorious whimper. In the words of the narrator of <u>Gravity's Rainbow</u>, "When the mice run down, who knows tonight but what they've run for good?"[7]

NOTES

[1]Trans. Gregory Rabassa (New York: Harper, 1970), p. 422. Further references to this book will appear as page numbers in the text.

[2]Cleveland and New York: World, 1956.

[3]William F. Arndt and F. Wilbur Gingrich, <u>A Greek-English Lexicon of the New Testament</u> (Chicago: Univ. of Chicago Press, 1957), p. 72.

[4]Demetrio Aguilera-Malta, <u>Siete lunas y siete serpientes</u> (Mexico City: Fondo de Cultura Economica, 1970), p. 120. Further references to this book will appear as page numbers in the text.

[5]Trans. Donald Gardner and Suzanne Jill Levine (New York: Harper, 1971). Since the translation is in reality a rewriting of the text, my page references are to the original <u>Tres tristes tigres</u> (Barcelona: Seix Barral, 1967).

[6]"Cantando las 40," supplement to <u>Imagen</u> 42 (1969), n.p.

[7]New York: Viking Compass, 1973, p. 37.

Index

Achilles, 11.

Adonis, 96, 99.

Agamemnon, 11.

Albee, Edward, 21-23;
"Art as Redemption of
the Absurd," 22.

Anácreon, 13.

Antonioni, Michelangelo,
20, 21, 103-11
passim.

Anouilh, Jean, 22.

Aguilera-Malta, 115,
116.

Ariadne, 59.

Aristotle, 16.

Arnold, Matthew, 4.

Artaud, Antonin, 81.

Attis, 96, 99, 100.

Barfield, Owen, 25.

Bastos, Roa, 115.

Bergman, Ingmar, 20.

Blackwood, Algernon,
27, 29, 30, 31, 32.

Blake, William, 53.

Boccaccio, Giovanni, 19.

Breton, André, 81.

Browning, Elisabeth
Barrett, 18.

Buñuel, Luis, 82.

Burgess, Anthony, 67.

Cabrera, Guillermo, 119.

Caesar, Julius, 52.

Campbell, Joseph, 25, 32,
53, 55, 116.

Camus, Albert, 12, 23.

Canudo, Ricardo, 35, 41.

Carpentier, Alejo, 115.

Cary, Joseph, 67.

Christianity, 6, 19;
"Christian-Hebraic
Legacy," 8.

Cocteau, Jean, 82.

123